The Old Farmer's ALMANAC for Kids

VOLUME 6

YANKEE PUBLISHING
INCORPORATED

――――

The Old Farmer's Almanac Books

Publisher: Sherin Pierce

Series editor: Janice Stillman
Art director: Colleen Quinnell
Copy editor: Jack Burnett
Contributors: Jack Burnett, Alice Cary, Tim Clark, Sharon Criscoe, Mare-Anne Jarvela, Barbara Mills Lasonde, Margo Letourneau, Martie Majoros, Susan Peery, Sarah Perreault, Stephanie Shaw, Heidi Stonehill

V.P., new media and production: Paul Belliveau
Production directors: Susan Gross, David Ziarnowski
Production artists: Lucille Rines, Rachel Kipka, Janet Grant

Companion Web site: Almanac4kids.com

Web editor: Catherine Boeckmann
Web designers: Lou S. Eastman, Amy O'Brien
E-commerce manager: Alan Henning
Programming: Reinvented, Inc.

For additional information about this and other publications from *The Old Farmer's Almanac,* visit **Almanac.com** or call **800-ALMANAC** (800-256-2622)

Consumer marketing manager: Kate McPherson

Distributed in the book trade in the United States by Houghton Mifflin Harcourt and in Canada by Thomas Allen & Son Limited

Direct-to-retail and bulk sales are handled by Stacey Korpi, 800-895-9265, ext. 160

Yankee Publishing Inc., P.O. Box 520, 1121 Main Street, Dublin, New Hampshire 03444

ISBN: 978-1-57198-683-2
ISSN: 1948-061X

FIRST PRINTING OF VOLUME 6

Thank you to everyone who had a hand in producing this Almanac and getting it to market, including printers, distributors, and sales and delivery people.

―――――――

PRINTED IN THE UNITED STATES OF AMERICA

HI, KIDS,

and Moms, Dads, Aunts, Uncles, Grandparents, and Teachers everywhere!

Welcome to *The Old Farmer's Almanac for Kids!* Here's what you will find inside:

- fascinating **facts** you won't believe
- entertaining **stories** to share
- cool **activities** to test your skills

- easy and delicious **recipes** to try
- amazing **tales** of kids' accomplishments
- challenging **games** and **quizzes**
- garden **ideas** to get you growing
- useful **information** that you'll remember for a lifetime

We hope that you enjoy every word on every page—and we'd love to know if you do (or don't)! Send us your thoughts, opinions, ideas, and impressions at **Almanac4kids.com/TellUs.** Or mail a letter to *The Old Farmer's Almanac for Kids,* **P.O. Box 520, Dublin, NH 03444.** Thanks for buying this book. We want the next one to be even better!

NOW, TURN THE PAGE, AND LET THE FUN BEGIN!

The Almanac Editors

CONTENTS

CALENDAR

ASTRONOMY

WEATHER

IN THE GARDEN

ON THE FARM

ACCOMPLISHED KIDS

NATURE

CONTENTS

FOOD

HEALTH

WILD ADVENTURERS

HISTORY

SPORTS

USEFUL & AMUSING

the birth of the

birthday party

a slice through layers of history

In ancient times, ordinary people seldom observed their birthday. Only rulers and their sons celebrated. In Egypt, birthdays were like holidays. Pharaohs and queens had parties, and citizens feasted at home.

In Rome, every man got to celebrate his birthday. (Women and children were considered unimportant.) The Romans were the first to make rulers' birthdays annual holidays. Some were marked by parades and banquets.

By the 4th century, townspeople began to keep a record of the days on which citizens were born. Before long, parties thrown by family and friends on each person's special day became common.

By the early 1800s, kids were having formal birthday parties, with games and dances. However, the idea was not for the children to have fun, but for them to be able to practice their manners.

It was not until after the Civil War (1861–65), when kitchen stoves became common appliances, that layered cakes became birthday treats.

CALENDAR

birthday customs

Thank the Germans for these traditions:

● **Candles:** A child's birthday party, or *Kinderfeste,* began at dawn, when he or she woke up to a cake with lighted candles. These stayed lit all day, even if this meant replacing some.

● **Making a wish before blowing out the candles in one breath:** People believed that the smoke carried the wish to heaven.

the birth of a song

The birthday song was written by sisters Mildred and Patty Smith. Patty was a teacher and later became a principal. Mildred pursued her love of music.

The sisters collaborated on several songs and in 1893 published *Song Stories for the Kindergarten,* which included this song:

> **Good morning to you,**
> **Good morning to you,**
> **Good morning, dear children,**
> **Good morning to all.**

Later, the song changed to "Happy birthday to you" instead of "Good morning to you." It's not known who made the change, but soon the song was being heard in theaters and other places and in "singing telegrams." This activity got the attention of Patty and Mildred's sister Jessica. She was concerned about protecting the family's rights to the song, so she had it copyrighted in 1935. This means that no one is allowed to use the song in a show, movie, or other business without paying for the use of it. **Don't worry: There is no charge to sing it at family parties and the like.**

try these cuts

To get more portions from a round or square cake, try cutting slices this way:

find a birthday

The founder of *The Old Farmer's Almanac*, Robert B. Thomas, was born on April 24, 1766.

To learn who's having—or had—a birthday on any day, go to the Birthday Finder on Almanac4kids.com.

let's have cake!

Birthdays are a great reason to make a special cake, but who needs a reason to have cake? Each of these recipes will turn any day into a celebration! To guarantee good results, ask an adult for help.

ROOT BEER CAKE

CAKE:

2 cups sugar

¼ cup shortening

3 cups all-purpose flour

6 tablespoons cornstarch

2 teaspoons baking powder

1 teaspoon salt

1 cup root beer

1 teaspoon root beer extract

5 egg whites, at room temperature

FROSTING:

1 cup heavy cream

¾ cup confectioners' sugar

1 teaspoon root beer extract

Preheat the oven to 350°F. Grease and flour two 9-inch round cake pans.

For cake: In a large mixing bowl, beat together the sugar and shortening until light and creamy.

In a separate bowl, sift together the flour, cornstarch, baking powder, and salt, then add this to the creamed mixture. Stir lightly. Add the root beer and root beer extract and beat well.

In a separate bowl, whip the egg whites until stiff. Carefully fold the egg whites into the cake batter.

Pour the batter into the prepared cake pans. Bake for 35 minutes, or until a toothpick inserted into the centers comes out clean. Cool the cake layers in the pans for 10 minutes before turning them out onto wire racks to cool. When the layers are completely cool, frost them.

For frosting: In a large bowl, combine the cream, sugar, and root beer extract, then use an electric mixer to beat until firm.

Makes 8 servings.

CHOCOLATE LAVA CAKE

½ cup (1 stick) plus 2 tablespoons
    unsalted butter, cut into large pieces
6 ounces bittersweet chocolate,
    broken into pieces
1 teaspoon vanilla extract
2 tablespoons sugar
3 large eggs plus 1 large yolk,
    at room temperature
1½ cups confectioners' sugar
½ cup all-purpose flour
big pinch of salt
vanilla ice cream, for topping

Combine all of the butter and the
chocolate in a microwave-safe bowl and cook
for 30 seconds at a time, stopping to stir the mixture,
until all of the chocolate has melted. Stir to smooth. Set aside to cool for
15 minutes. Stir in the vanilla.

Meanwhile, preheat the oven to 450°F. Butter six 1-cup ceramic ramekins.
Put 1 teaspoon of sugar into each ramekin. Turn and tilt the ramekins to
coat them evenly with sugar. Set aside.

Whisk the eggs and yolk in a large bowl. Add the confectioners' sugar and
stir to combine. (The mixture will look curdled.) Add the chocolate to the egg
mixture and stir well. Add the flour and salt, then stir well. Divide the batter
evenly among the ramekins, filling each about halfway.

Bake on the center oven rack for 9 to 11 minutes. When done, the cake will
have doubled in height; the top will be almost flat, not sunken; and a "skin"
will have formed around a soft center. Using a spatula and oven mitts,
remove the dishes from the oven. Place a dessert plate over each ramekin
and invert the cakes onto the plates. Wait about 10 seconds, then carefully
lift the ramekins. You should have a nicely shaped cake that will be slightly
sunken in the middle with a soft, lavalike center.

Serve right away, or cover the cakes with plastic wrap and refrigerate
on the plates. When ready to serve, reheat each one in the microwave for
10 to 15 seconds. Serve with a scoop of vanilla ice cream on top.
Makes 6 servings.

YOU'RE A

JANUARY

GARNET

The word "garnet" comes from the Latin word *granatum*, meaning pomegranate. Garnet is often the "sand" on sandpaper and occurs in almost every color except blue.

Garnets form in layers of rocks deep underground.

FEBRUARY

AMETHYST

Italian Renaissance artist and scientist Leonardo da Vinci believed that wearing an amethyst could make a person smarter.

Amethysts are a type of quartz often found in the geodes formed from cooled lava. They exist in many shades of purple.

MAY

EMERALD

Green emeralds were favorite gems of Cleopatra of ancient Egypt and Catherine the Great, empress of Russia.

Emeralds, like aquamarine, are a form of the mineral beryl.

JUNE

PEARL

Pearls can be as small as the head of a pin or as large as a pigeon egg.

Natural pearls form when a particle like a grain of sand gets inside the shell of an oyster and causes an irritation. Because it can not get rid of the particle, the oyster covers it with a substance called nacre.

SEPTEMBER

SAPPHIRE

In the 15th century, it was thought that holding a sapphire near a spider would kill the spider.

Synthetic sapphires can be made into "sapphire glass" that is used in barcode scanners like those at supermarket checkouts.

OCTOBER

OPAL

"Opal" comes from the Greek word *opallios*, meaning to see a change in color. When light hits an opal, the colors of the spectrum become visible.

Australian aboriginal tribes believed that opals were the Creator's footprints on Earth.

GEM!

Centuries ago, people assigned a gemstone to each month. Today, we call these gems birthstones. **WHAT'S YOURS?**

MARCH

AQUAMARINE

This stone's name comes from *aqua*, meaning water, and *mare*, meaning sea.

Sailors once wore aquamarine stones carved with the image of Neptune, the Roman god of the seas, to protect them during their travels.

APRIL

DIAMOND

Ancient Romans first associated diamonds with romance, believing that Cupid's arrows had diamonds on the tips.

Diamond contains tightly formed carbon crystals, making it the hardest mineral on Earth.

JULY

RUBY

One of the largest rubies is called the "Peace" ruby because it was found in 1919, shortly after World War I had ended.

Rubies' color may range from deep red (sometimes called pigeon's blood) to pale rose. Blue rubies are known as sapphires.

AUGUST

PERIDOT

The largest peridot (PARE-a-dot or PARE-a-doe) ever found weighs 319 carats (2.3 ounces). It is in the Smithsonian Institution in Washington, D.C.

Yellow-green peridot has been found in volcanic lava in Hawaii and in meteorites that have fallen to Earth.

NOVEMBER

TOPAZ

The word "topaz" may come from the Sanskrit word for "fire," or it may be named for the island of Topazios in the Red Sea. Topaz is clear in its purest form.

Yellow-brown topaz is harder than quartz. It is often used in dishware and as insulation for spark plugs.

DECEMBER

TURQUOISE
(sometimes Zircon)

Turquoise has been set in jewelry since about 6000 B.C., when Egyptians first mined it. Native Americans in the U.S. Southwest also use it in jewelry.

Turquoise is found most often in desert areas where volcanic activity has occurred.

EVERYTHING
YOU NEED TO KNOW
ABOUT
EASTER

WHY "EASTER"?

The name may have derived from the Saxon goddess Eostre, whose feast day was celebrated each spring. Or it may have derived from the word *oster*, meaning "rising."

WHAT IS EASTER?

Centuries ago, Easter was one of the earliest—if not *the* earliest—of the annual festivals celebrating spring and new life.

Today, it is the day on which Christians remember the resurrection, or rising, of Christ after His crucifixion.

March 2016

Sunday	Monday	Tuesday	Wednesday	Thursday	Friday	Saturday
		1	2	3	4	5
6	7	8	9	10	11	12
13	14	15	16	17	18	19
20	21	22	23	24	25	26
27	28	29	30	31		

WHEN IS EASTER?

Easter can occur as early as March 22 and as late as April 25, according to the western Christian church. (Eastern and western churches usually celebrate Easter on a different day.)

WHY IS IT ALWAYS ON A DIFFERENT SUNDAY?

The date for Easter is determined through a complicated formula based on the full Moon that occurs on or shortly after March 21. The original calculations were made in the year 325 and did not consider all factors of lunar motion, so Easter may differ from the actual full Moon date by a day or so.

ABOUT THE MOON

The Easter full Moon (as calculated by Christian churches) is often called the Paschal full Moon. The word "paschal" stems from the Hebrew word *pesach*, which refers to the Passover feast, a festival of redemption. Before there was a Passover feast, people celebrated the arrival of spring and the passing of winter.

WHY DO PEOPLE LIGHT BONFIRES?

Some Germans have an ancient tradition of lighting bonfires on the night before Easter to symbolize the end of winter and beginning of spring.

WHY IS THERE AN EASTER BUNNY?

In folklore, the Easter bunny recalls the hare, the Egyptian symbol of birth and fertility.

WHY DO WE HAVE EASTER EGGS?

For centuries, the egg has represented rebirth. People from many cultures noticed that when winter came to an end, the earth would burst forth with plant life, just as a chick or baby bird bursts through an eggshell.

For Ukrainians, the egg yolk represented the Sun. They also valued eggs because they produced roosters, which, Ukrainians believed, called the Sun to rise every morning by crowing.

IF IT RAINS ON EASTER DAY, THERE SHALL BE GOOD GRASS BUT VERY LITTLE HAY.

THE BEST EGGS FOR DECORATING

White eggs (of chicken breeds such as the Ancona, California White, Minorca, or Leghorn) are the best, although brown eggs (from the Rhode Island Red, White Rock, Golden Comet, New Hampshire Red, and Plymouth Rock breeds) are fine, too.

"PRE-DECORATED" EGGS

Araucana hens lay eggs with a pastel blue, marbleized appearance.
The Araucana is sometimes mistakenly called the "Easter Egg Chicken."

THE FIRST WHITE HOUSE EASTER EGG ROLL TOOK PLACE ON APRIL 22, 1878.

WHITE HOUSE
EASTER EGG ROLL

SAVE THE SHELLS!

Dispose of eggshells in the compost pile. As they decompose, they add valuable nutrients to garden soil.

FRACTURED FOLKLORE

One of the oddest Easter customs was lifting, or heaving, practiced in the Victorian period (mid-1800s). On Easter Monday (the day after Easter), a man could take hold of and lift any woman off the ground and kiss her. On Easter Tuesday, ladies got their turn to lift and kiss any man. The practice fell out of favor when people began to object to being lifted.

HOW TO DYE EGGS

To help prevent eggs from cracking in hot water, bring them to room temperature before boiling. See also the tip opposite.

Buy a dye kit and follow the directions on it or use natural coloring (the more you use, the stronger the colors will be). Here's how:

1. Place the egg or eggs in a pot.
2. Add enough cool water to cover, plus 2 tablespoons of vinegar.
3. Add one of these vegetables, fruit, or spices:
   - red cabbage (coarsely chopped), blueberries or blackberries (crushed), or grape juice for blue color
   - spinach or parsley for green color
   - chili powder or paprika for orange color
   - beets (grated or canned with juice), cherries, cranberries, or pomegranate juice for red or pink color
   - yellow onion skins, ground cumin, ground turmeric, or lemon or orange peels for yellow color
4. Put the pot on the stove.
5. Set the heat on high to bring the water to a boil.
6. When the water boils, cover the pot with a tight-fitting lid, turn off the heat, and let the pot stand for 25 minutes.

HOW TO AVOID CRACKING THE SHELL WHEN BOILING AN EGG

Using a sewing needle, safety pin, or pushpin, puncture the fat bottom end of the egg so that it will be less likely to crack while boiling. Push just hard enough to make a hole in the shell; go too deep, and the white will leak out and solidify while cooking.

OOOPS!

If an egg cracks while boiling, immediately lower the heat and pour a large quantity of salt on the crack. This will often seal it and stop a lot of the egg white from escaping.

GO FOR A SPIN

To determine which eggs in the refrigerator are raw and which are hard-boiled, spin each egg on its fat end. A raw egg won't spin as fast as a cooked egg.

(And next time, mark an X on your hard-boiled eggs!)

Why Do We **LEAP** Years?

A leap year is one with 366 days. A non–leap year has 365 days. The extra day is added to the shortest month, February, to give it 29 days (one day more than its usual 28 days). The 29th day is called Leap Day.

LEAP *Laws*

A leap year is one that is divisible by four, such as 2016.

An end-of-the-century year also must be divisible by 400 to be a leap year. 2000 was a leap year, but 1900 was not.

WHY IT COUNTS

If we didn't leap, the calendar would be off by 5 hours, 48 minutes, and 45 seconds each year.

One orbit of Earth around the Sun takes 365.2422 days. Adding an extra day to the calendar helps to make it match the four seasons.

But it's not a perfect match: Adding a leap day every 4 years overcompensates by a few extra seconds each leap year, adding up to about 3 extra days every 10,000 years.

TRACKING TIME

● The word for adding an extra day, week, or month to the calendar is "intercalation."

● Every year, January 1 and December 31 fall on the same day of the week, unless it's a leap year.

● The longest amount of time possible between consecutive leap years is **8 years.** The next time this happens is between 2096 and 2104.

● Since 1971, one leap second has been added to the calendar about once every 18 months, at midnight on either December 31 or June 30.

Years ago, babies born on Leap Day had their birthdays recorded on February 28 or March 1. Today, anybody born on February 29 is called a "leapling" (or a "29er"), and this day is his or her birthday. About 4 million people in the world are leaplings.

HOW *Old Are You* NOW?

Leaplings sometimes calculate their age in leap years. For example, in 2017, a person born on February 29, 1996, might say that he or she is 5 years old. It's not true. This person would be 21 years old.

BELIEVE IT OR NOT . . .

☞ The Estes family of Utah has three leaplings. Louise Estes gave birth to Xavier in 2004, Remington in 2008, and Jade in 2012—all on leap days!

☞ The Leap Year Capital of the World is a town named Anthony that is half in Texas and half in New Mexico. Every leap year, the town celebrates with a festival that was started by two leaplings.

Calling All Leaplings!

On what day do you celebrate your birthday in non–leap years?

Share at Almanac4kids.com/TellUs/Leaplings.

ALMANAC ODDITIES

For centuries, people have marked certain days with **practices, rituals, sayings,** and **folklore.** Some are well known, some are obscure, and some no longer exist, but all give a glimpse into our multicultural heritage. Note these **facts, legends,** and **curiosities** throughout the year.

January 1: **New Year's Day**

According to Armenian-American storytellers, at midnight on New Year's Eve, rivers and streams around the world stopped flowing for the first 5 minutes of the new year. People who visited the water source when it began to flow again would discover gold dust, not water, flowing from it for a few seconds.

The First Monday After January 6: **Plough Monday**

"Plough" is an alternate spelling of the farmer's tilling tool, the plow. On this day, the first Monday after the 12 days following Christmas (which end on January 6), farmers returned to their labors.

January 7: **Distaff Day**

A distaff is a tool used when spinning wool. This day marked the end of the Christmas celebration, when women returned to their normal chores. For many, this included spinning wool to be woven or knit into garments.

February 2: **Groundhog Day**

Traditionally, February 2 was the day when farmers tried to determine the weather for the next 6 weeks. They believed that if an animal came out of hibernation on this day and saw its shadow, winter would continue. (If the animal did not see its shadow, mild weather would follow.) For centuries, farmers in France and England looked to a bear for this sign; in Germany, they kept their eye on the badger. In the 1800s, German immigrants to Pennsylvania brought the tradition with them. Finding no badgers, they adopted the groundhog to fit the lore.

February 14: **Valentine's Day**

In some parts of the U.S. South, communities held Pound Suppers. Every boy brought a pound of something for dinner. Girls put their names into a hat. Each boy pulled a name and then carried the girl whose name he drew to the dinner table for supper.

March 3: **Dolls' Festival**

On the third day of the third month, Japanese girls set up a table in the corner of a room. On it, they place a series of shelves covered with red fabric or carpet. On the top shelf, the girls place emperor and empress dolls. On the shelf below, ladies-in-waiting dolls; below them, court musician dolls, each with an instrument. Other dolls, plus doll-size furnishings, are placed on lower shelves. All of the dolls are dressed in traditional costumes. On a separate table, the girls place cookies, cakes, and rice cakes. Girls visit each other's doll displays and have tea parties. They may receive gifts of dolls from family and friends.

April's First Monday: **Tater Day**

Tater Day began in Benton, Kentucky, in 1842 as a market day, when farmers would sell or buy sweet "tater" (potato) shoots for the next growing season and swap mules. Over the years, it grew into a weekend event, with a carnival, food, parade, and more.

May 1: **May Day**

This day is celebrated with the crowning of a May queen and dancing and singing around a Maypole that is decorated with flowers. Other traditions are planting watermelon seeds before sunrise and going fishing. Folklore says that if you catch a fish today, you will catch fish every day in May.

May 5: **Boys' Festival or Children's Day**

Similarly to Dolls' Festival (March 3), Japanese boys display soldier, warrior, and hero dolls in costume and with swords and bows and arrows. Bamboo poles, set outside the home, bear brightly colored streamers and paper or cloth carp (fish), a symbol of energy and courage. The carp seem to swim in the wind. Boys spend the day acting out the battles of ancient warriors.

Mid-June: **Turtle Days**

In 1898, Oscar Fulk, a farmer in Churubusco, Indiana, claimed that a giant snapping turtle lived in his lake. People named the turtle Oscar, after Fulk. Fifty years later, farmer Gale Harris claimed to have seen the turtle, too. He tried all kinds of ways to catch it, including pumping out the lake. Eventually, tales of the "Beast of 'Busco" (that's what folks called the turtle) brought attention to the town, so they decided to celebrate with a festival—Turtle Days weekend.

June 24: **Midsummer Day**

In Buffalo, New York, children were not allowed to go swimming until this day every summer. (Parents believed it unsafe to do so.)

In Europe, Ukrainian girls at summer camps made little boats, decorated them with flowers, and outfitted them with candles, which they lit before launching their craft onto lakes and streams.

July 3 to August 11: **Dog Days**

These 40 days are traditionally the hottest days of the year. A long time ago, on these days the Dog Star (Sirius) rose at the same time as the Sun. Ancient folks believed that the extreme hot weather was caused by the star and the Sun together.

August 15: **Our Lady of the Flowers**

On this religious feast day, Polish-American children each brought a bouquet of flowers, an apple, and a carrot to church to be blessed. After returning home, they set the flowers aside to dry. When ready, the goods would be placed in the attic to prevent lightning from striking the house.

Late September: **Harvest Home**

Around the time of the autumn equinox, the harvest was finished and people celebrated with feasts, fun, and thanksgiving. Being at the end of the summer season, it was also the time to pay workers, collect rents, and hold elections.

September or October: **Full Moon**

The Chinese Midautumn Festival, which is more than 3,000 years old, occurs on the fall's largest full Moon and honors the Moon and the harvest. People light lanterns and exchange and eat small Moon cakes, while gazing at the Moon. Traditional cake fillings include egg yolk (a symbol of the Moon), lotus seed paste, and five kernels (nuts and seeds).

October or November: **Double Ninth Day**

According to Chinese legend, a farmer was warned that a disaster would occur on the ninth day of the ninth lunar month, and, to escape it, he needed to move to higher ground. He took his family into the mountains and thus survived. Today, this day is also called the Festival of High Places. Families fly kites, which they believe carry away bad luck, and eat nine-layer cakes.

October 31: **Halloween**

Apple bobbing began with the ancient Romans: The first person to catch an apple in his or her teeth was believed to be the first who would marry in that year.

Vegetable carving originated with the ancient Irish, who cut faces into turnips and potatoes. They started carving pumpkins when they came to America.

Trick-or-treating originated in the Middle Ages, when wealthy people gave poor people "soul cakes" (baked goods) if they promised to pray for the rich people's dead family members.

November: **Lobsters move to offshore waters**

Every November, lobsters migrate from shallow waters about 30 feet deep near land to depths of up to 50 feet deep in order to escape the stormy seas that winter brings. Depending on their age and variety, lobsters migrate from 5 miles to as much as almost 20 miles to find calmer, relatively warmer waters. Spiny lobsters, the ones that do not have large claws, have been seen lining up in single file and marching across the ocean floor. Large-claw, or American, lobsters have never been seen migrating, but they have been caught, tagged, and released, and their migrations have been tracked electronically. Through this, researchers in the 1980s learned that one lobster had traveled more than 900 miles in 3½ years!

Mid-December: **Halcyon Days**

Ancient Greeks and Romans experienced about 2 weeks of calm weather every year in mid-December, often around the winter solstice. They believed that at this time, the colorful kingfisher, or halcyon, cared for its young in nests on or near the sea. Legend said that the bird calmed the wind and waves and thus brought fine weather.

December 25: **Christmas**

In Tennessee, it was once believed that a baby born on Christmas day could understand the speech of animals.

In North Carolina, some folks believed that if you washed clothes within 3 weeks of Christmas, you would "wash someone out of your family"—cause a family member to die.

Folks who burned a Yule log would save a portion to burn in the new year, in hope of protecting the house from a lightning strike.

How to Find Week for

You can determine the day of the week for any date as far back as 1753 and as far ahead as 2099, without a calendar. **HERE'S HOW: Pick a date. Let's use** March 25, 1913, **the day of the Dayton, Ohio, flood.**

1

Divide the last two digits of the year (13) by 4 (13/4 = 3, with 1 remaining). 3 is the quotient; discard any remainder (1).

2

Note the day of the month (25).

3

Go to Month Keys Table and get the Month Key (March = 4).

4

Add the last two digits of the year, the quotient, the day of the month, and the Month Key: 13 + 3 + 25 + 4 = 45. This is the Sum.

5

Divide the Sum (45) by 7 (45/7 = 6, with 3 remaining).

6

Using the remainder (3), go to the Day Keys Table to find the day of the week. The flood took place on a Tuesday.

STOP!

- If the year is before 1800, add 4 to the Sum before dividing.
- If the year is from 1800 through 1899, add 2 to the Sum before dividing.
- If the year is from 2000 through 2099, subtract 1 from the Sum before dividing.

the Day of the Any Date

MONTH KEYS TABLE

January	I	June	5
When January is in a leap year	0	July	0
February	4	August	3
When February is in a leap year	3	September	6
March	4	October	I
April	0	November	4
May	2	December	6

DAY KEYS TABLE

Saturday	0
Sunday	I
Monday	2
Tuesday	3
Wednesday	4
Thursday	5
Friday	6

Find the Day of the Week of These Events

I. April 24, 1766, when *Old Farmer's Almanac* founder Robert B. Thomas was born

2. September 26, 1820, when frontiersman Daniel Boone died

3. August 12, 1936, when 13-year-old diver Marjorie Gestring won an Olympic gold medal

4. May 8, 2004, when Bandit, said to be the world's heaviest raccoon at 75 pounds, died

"FIND THE DAY" ANSWERS

1. April 24, 1766, was a Thursday. The math: 66 + 16 + 24 + 0 + 4 = 110; 110/7 = 15 with a remainder of 5.

2. September 26, 1820, was a Tuesday. The math: 20 + 5 + 26 + 6 + 2 = 59; 59/7 = 8 with a remainder of 3.

3. August 12, 1936, was a Wednesday. The math: 36 + 9 + 12 + 3 = 60; 60/7 = 8 with a remainder of 4.

4. May 8, 2004, was a Saturday. The math: 04 + 1 + 8 + 2 − 1 = 14; 14/7 = 2 with no remainder.

The Newest EYE in the SKY

In 2018, our view of outer space will change dramatically. That's the expected launch year for the James Webb Space Telescope (JWST), a large, space-based observatory. It's being built by the U.S.'s National Aeronautics and Space Administration (NASA), the European Space

ASTRONOMY

Countdown
for the
next space
telescope

A life-size model of the
James Webb Space Telescope
on display in Austin, Texas

Agency, and the Canadian Space Agency. Considered
the successor to the Hubble Space Telescope, which has
been providing fantastic images of galaxies since 1990,
the JWST will look further back in time to see inside dust
clouds, where stars and planet systems are forming today.

INFRA MAGIC

An infrared device, such as a camera, detects the heat generated by a person, animal, or thing and can "see" the object from which the heat emanates. In this way, the JWST can detect light from young stars that are hidden in clouds and dust.

THE EXPANDING COOKIE UNIVERSE

The universe is always changing. Galaxies keep moving farther apart. Think of it as a chocolate chip cookie. As the cookie dough bakes, rises, and spreads, the chips move farther apart.

Humble HUBBLE

Edwin Hubble, for whom the Hubble Space Telescope is named, discovered that the farther a galaxy is from Earth, the faster it appears to move away. This idea of an "expanding universe" has been expanding ever since— and its study is one of the missions of the JWST.

THE SPACEWIDE WEBB

James Webb, for whom the JWST is named, was the head of NASA in the 1960s and inspired NASA's space program, culminating in the landing on the Moon.

Scope It Out!

Learn more about the JWST and tube-shape telescopes by playing Scope It Out! at http://jwst.nasa.gov/scope.html.

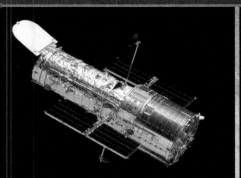
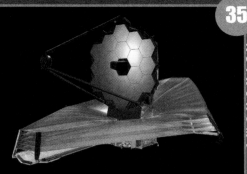

Hubble Telescope vs. Webb Telescope

The Hubble's single, solid, light-gathering **mirror** is about 94½ inches in diameter.	The JWST will have **18 mirrors** that measure a total of 256 inches in diameter, providing seven times more light-gathering power than the Hubble.
The Hubble's orbit is about **355 miles above Earth.**	The JWST will be **932,000 miles away.**
The Hubble is **43½ feet long and 8 feet wide,** about the size of a school bus.	The JWST is about **72 feet by 39 feet**, almost the size of a tennis court, which is 78 feet by 26 feet. It will be folded up, like origami (the Japanese paper-folding technique), for launch.
The Hubble would be able to **see a 12" beach ball from 375 miles away.**	The JWST's **telescope** is so powerful that it would be able to **see a penny from 24 miles away.** The JWST will have infrared instrumentation, allowing it to see longer wavelengths of light with greater sensitivity than the Hubble.
The Hubble **orbits Earth.**	The JWST will **orbit the Sun,** always in the same spot in relation to Earth and the Sun. The solar shield on the JWST's telescope will keep it cool by blocking the light from the Sun, Earth, and Moon. The **telescope** must be kept at −400°F to operate properly.
The Hubble was **launched by a Space Shuttle,** part of a program that has been discontinued.	The JWST will be **launched on an Ariane 5 rocket** from the European Spaceport near Kourou, French Guiana. It will separate from the rocket 30 minutes after launch. More than 1,000 people in more than 17 countries are contributing to its success.

OH, MY STARS!

 Nebula means "cloud" in Latin.

 A nebula is a cloud of gas and dust in space.

 More than one nebula are called nebulae.

Nebulae are areas in which new stars are formed or stars have died or are dying. There are four basic types of nebulae:

EMISSION NEBULAE are the most colorful. They are lit from the inside by new stars.

★ ★ ★ ★ ★ ★

REFLECTION NEBULAE reflect starlight from inside or near themselves.

★ ★ ★ ★ ★ ★

DARK NEBULAE produce no visible light themselves; they block light and are apparent in silhouette.

★ ★ ★ ★ ★ ★

PLANETARY NEBULAE result when remnants of stars shed their outer layers, throwing off dust and gas.

The Hubble Space Telescope has imaged dozens of nebulae by combining many smaller pictures into mosaics such as those at right. Each nebula is given a number. Some are given names based on the thing that they most resemble to observers. Match the name of each nebula with its image.

CAT'S EYE was one of the first planetary nebulae to be discovered and is one of the most complex.

BUTTERFLY, also known as the Bug, formed when a star about five times the size of the Sun ejected its outer layers.

CONE is a star-forming pillar that resembles a beast rising from a crimson sea.

BOOMERANG consists of two nearly symmetric lobes of matter ejected from a central star.

HORSEHEAD resembles a horse rising out of a sea of dust and gas.

ANT has fiery lobes that resemble the insect's head and thorax.

WITCH HEAD is a profile, with eye, nose, open mouth, and pointed chin.

MONKEY HEAD, in profile, is where stars are being formed.

TARANTULA is the bright, spiderlike home to thousands of massive stars.

NECKLACE is dotted with bright knots of gas that resemble diamonds.

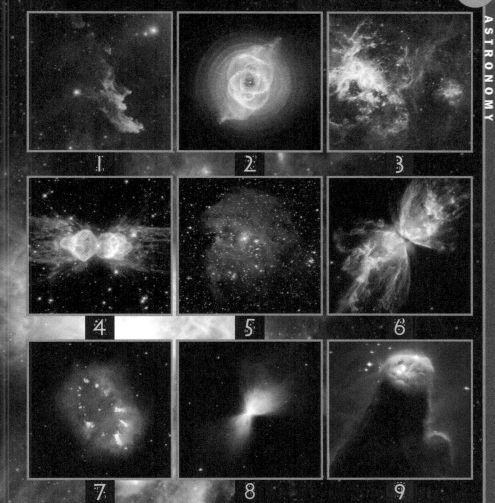

What happens when a cloud touches the ground?

Fog!

Fog makes for mysterious weather. Like smoke, it can suddenly fill the air, making things nearly impossible to see. It can be eerie, it can be hazardous, but it's not a mystery.

Fog is a cloud that forms close to the ground. Fog can form only when both water vapor and millions of tiny particles (think dust) are present in the air. The water vapor turns to liquid water that clings to the particles—in a process called "condensation"—to produce fog. Sea fog forms around particles of salt from the ocean. Fog is heavier and thicker than mist, because foggy air contains more water droplets.

FOG TALK

● Have you ever felt confused? The expression for this is "in a fog."

● A heavy fog that forms when water condenses around tiny coal particles in the air is often described as "thick as pea soup." This fog is brownish yellow, like pea soup. London became famous for these fogs in the mid-1900s because so many factories and homes burned coal for energy.

Fog

*The fog comes
on little cat feet.*

*It sits looking
over harbor and city
on silent haunches
and then moves on.*

–Carl Sandburg, American poet
(1878–1967)

Hear Sandburg read his famous poem
at http://tinyurl.com/Sandburg-fog.

- Along the east coast of Scotland, fog is called *haar,* or North Sea *haar.*

- Along the east coast of England, fog is called *fret,* or sea *fret.*

- Ice fog that forms in mountain valleys of the U.S. West is called pogonip.

- Fog that forms in San Joaquin Valley, California, is called tule.

How Fog Feels

Think of a hot day. Did you feel damp and did the air seem heavy? If so, it was probably because the warm air contained a lot of water vapor. You were surrounded by tiny, floating water molecules.

The warmer the air, the more water it can hold. We call the level of water vapor in the air "humidity" and say that a hot, sticky day with lots of water vapor is "humid."

Cool air holds less water. Think of a day when the air feels crisp and fresh.

FOGGIEST PLACES

ON EARTH: Grand Banks, off the coast of Newfoundland, Canada, where the cold Labrador ocean current meets the much warmer Gulf Stream. Nearby Saint John's has about 2,900 hours of fog per year.

ON THE U.S. EAST COAST: Moose Peak Lighthouse on Mistake Island, Maine, with an average of 1,600 hours of fog per year.

ON THE U.S. WEST COAST: Cape Disappointment, Washington, with an average of 2,550 hours of fog a year.

ADVECTION FOG occurs when warm, moist air flows over cooler air that is closer to the ground. The Pacific coast of the United States is often covered in advection fog. Sea fog is always advection fog.

FLASH FOG is fog that forms (and disappears) suddenly.

RADIATION FOG forms in the evening when heat absorbed by the ground during the day radiates into the air. It usually occurs in winter, under clear, calm skies, and often burns off in the morning sun. Some people call it "ground fog."

FREEZING FOG occurs when fog droplets freeze on solid surfaces, such as mountaintops. The fog droplets are supercooled, or below the normal freezing point yet still liquid.

ICE FOG forms when ice crystals are in the air. This typically happens in arctic climates, in temperatures of 14°F or colder.

VALLEY FOG forms when dense, moist air gets trapped in mountain valleys, often in winter.

FOG CATCHERS

Water is scarce for people living high in the hills surrounding Lima, Peru. However, fog from the Pacific Ocean is plentiful from June through November, so the people catch it in nets.

With the help of scientists, villagers in the hillside village of Bellavista, Peru, have set up fog nets to catch

tiny water droplets in the air when wind blows fog in. The drops eventually flow through tubes to a collecting pool. One net has collected more than 600 gallons in a day.

Also, a nonprofit Canadian group called FogQuest sets up fog collectors in villages around the world.

Fatal Fog

The **London Fog** of 1952 killed about 4,000 people. The weather had been cold, causing Londoners to burn lots of coal to keep their homes warm. A high-pressure air mass prevented smoke from rising into the atmosphere. Instead, the smoke was trapped, along with pollution and gases from factories. The fog that formed was heavy, brown, and full of poisonous gases. When Londoners breathed this pollution, many got sick and died. England's Clean Air Act of 1956 helped to reduce the use of coal.

DESERT FOG

The **Atacama Desert,** high in the mountains of South America, is the driest place on Earth—too dry for most plants and animals. It may get 4 inches of precipitation every 1,000 years!

Luckily, fog appears more frequently. Locals call the fog that blows in from the Pacific Ocean *camanchaca,* and they use fog nets to collect its precious water.

WHY FOGHORNS BLOW LOW NOTES

Robert Foulis, an inventor and native of Scotland, was emigrating to the United States in 1818 when bad weather and rough seas forced his boat to harbor in Nova Scotia. Robert and his daughter stayed in Canada, later settling in New Brunswick.

One night, while walking home in thick fog, Robert heard his daughter playing the piano. He could hear the low notes that she played more clearly than the high notes. This sparked his imagination, and in 1853 he presented plans to the lighthouse commissioners for a steam-operated foghorn, the first of its kind, on Partridge Island in Saint John Harbor.

The harbor had been using a bell tower warning system, but Robert's invention produced long, low notes that were much easier to hear. It was installed in 1859 and used until 1998.

Unfortunately, an American had patented the foghorn, so Robert was unable to realize financial success from his idea. He died in 1866.

Q: What do you get if you cross water droplets with an amphibian?

A: Kermist the Fog!

FAMOUS FOGHORNS

Advection fog is so thick over San Francisco Bay that foghorns have been mounted on the **Golden Gate Bridge** since it opened in 1937. Thousands of boats have been safely guided by these horns. On average, they operate about 2½ hours each day. In August 1992, the foghorns blew for 15 days!

To hear the South Tower foghorn, go to http://tinyurl.com/SoundofFogHorn.

How to Measure Hail

The Torro Hailstorm Intensity Scale was introduced by Jonathan Webb
of Oxford, England, in 1986 as a means of categorizing hailstorms.
The name derives from the private and mostly British research body named
the TORnado and storm Research Organisation.

Intensity/Description of Hail Damage
H0 True hail of pea size causes no damage
H1 Leaves and flower petals are punctured and torn
H2 Leaves are stripped from trees and plants
H3 Panes of glass are broken; auto bodies are dented
H4 Some house windows are broken; small tree branches are broken off; birds are killed
H5 Many windows are smashed; small animals are injured; large tree branches are broken off
H6 Shingle roofs are breached; metal roofs are scored; wooden window frames are broken away
H7 Roofs are shattered to expose rafters; autos are seriously damaged
H8 Shingle and tile roofs are destroyed; small tree trunks are split; people are seriously injured
H9 Concrete roofs are broken; large tree trunks are split and knocked down; people are at risk of fatal injuries
H10 Brick houses are damaged; people are at risk of fatal injuries

The UV Index for Measuring Ultraviolet Radiation Risk

The U.S. National Weather Service's daily forecasts of ultraviolet levels
use these numbers for various exposure levels:

UV Index Number	Exposure Level	Time to Burn	Actions to Take
0, 1, 2	Minimal	60 minutes	Apply SPF 15 sunscreen
3, 4	Low	45 minutes	Apply SPF 15 sunscreen; wear a hat
5, 6	Moderate	30 minutes	Apply SPF 15 sunscreen; wear a hat
7, 8, 9	High	15–25 minutes	Apply SPF 15 to 30 sunscreen; wear a hat and sunglasses; limit midday exposure
10 or higher	Very high	10 minutes	Apply SPF 30 sunscreen; wear a hat, sunglasses, and protective clothing; limit midday exposure

"Time to Burn" and **"Actions to Take"** apply to people with fair skin
that sometimes tans but usually burns. People with lighter skin need to be more
cautious. People with darker skin may be able to tolerate more exposure.

How to Measure Wind Speed

The Beaufort Wind Force Scale is a common way of estimating wind speed. It was developed in 1805 by Admiral Sir Francis Beaufort of the British Navy to measure wind at sea. We can also use it to measure wind on land.

Admiral Beaufort arranged the numbers 0 to 12 to indicate the strength of the wind from calm, force 0, to hurricane, force 12. Here's a scale adapted to land.

"Used Mostly at Sea but of Help to All Who Are Interested in the Weather"

Beaufort Force	Description	When You See or Feel This Effect	Wind Speed (mph)	(km/h)
0	Calm	Smoke goes straight up	less than 1	less than 2
1	Light air	Wind direction is shown by smoke drift but not by wind vane	1–3	2–5
2	Light breeze	Wind is felt on the face; leaves rustle; wind vanes move	4–7	6–11
3	Gentle breeze	Leaves and small twigs move steadily; wind extends small flags straight out	8–12	12–19
4	Moderate breeze	Wind raises dust and loose paper; small branches move	13–18	20–29
5	Fresh breeze	Small trees sway; waves form on lakes	19–24	30–39
6	Strong breeze	Large branches move; wires whistle; umbrellas are difficult to use	25–31	40–50
7	Moderate gale	Whole trees are in motion; walking against the wind is difficult	32–38	51–61
8	Fresh gale	Twigs break from trees; walking against the wind is very difficult	39–46	62–74
9	Strong gale	Buildings suffer minimal damage; roof shingles are removed	47–54	75–87
10	Whole gale	Trees are uprooted	55–63	88–101
11	Violent storm	Widespread damage	64–72	102–116
12	Hurricane	Widespread destruction	73+	117+

WHEN NATURE FLAMES UP

WILDFIRES RESULT FROM AND CREATE UNIQUE WEATHER CONDITIONS.

Around the world each year, wildfires burn millions of acres of forest and grassland. The only continent spared from the wrath of fire is ice- and snow-covered Antarctica.

Wildfires are a product of the weather. Drought sets the stage for most major fires. The lack of rain dries the vegetation, making it ripe for ignition. Periodic drought affects almost all regions of the world.

Under the most extreme conditions, wildfires are unstoppable. A wall of flames, sometimes hundreds of feet high, marks the head of the fire. Wildfires can move at speeds exceeding 10 miles per hour and can easily overtake

someone on foot. Smoke can reduce visibility to next to nothing. A column of superheated air and smoke can rise for miles into the atmosphere above the fire.

Wind can turn a small fire into a big one, driving the flames forward at speeds that can easily outpace any type of control methods. When the combination of dryness and wind occurs, fire danger soars.

However, forest and grassland fires are part of nature's recycling process. Soon after a fire has seemingly destroyed an area, regrowth appears. Eventually, the forest or grassland will become mature again and the process will repeat itself.

HOW ARE WILDFIRES IGNITED?

■ By dry lightning strikes: In these cases, even if thunderstorms form, the rain from them evaporates in the dry air below before it reaches the ground.

■ By people accidentally, through campfires, sparks from power tools, and discarded cigarettes.

■ By burning debris and embers picked up by winds and dropped well ahead of the main fire.

SLAVE LAKE, ALBERTA

On this day at 3:00 P.M., Jamie Coutts, chief of the Lesser Slave Regional Fire Service, was keeping an eye on a wildfire that had started the day before about 10 miles south of the town of Slave Lake and been contained overnight. Then the winds picked up, blowing at 30 mph with gusts to near 44 mph. Within 30 minutes, the fire had crossed the highway and begun burning the town. In less than 12 hours, almost half of the town of Slave Lake was destroyed. This was considered to be the fastest-moving fire in the recorded history of Canada.

FIGHTING WORDS

☐ A wildfire that is **CONTAINED** is no longer advancing but is still burning vigorously behind the fire containment lines.

☐ A **PYROCUMULUS CLOUD** forms from rising air that carries ash upward, due to heat from wildfires or volcanic eruptions. Ash and smoke give the cloud a gray or brown color.

☐ **FIRE WHIRLS** are small tornadoes filled with burning debris.

WEATHER

Memorial service for the 19 members of the Granite Mountain Hotshot Team

☐ **DRY LIGHTNING** is a lightning strike that reaches the ground in the absence of any accompanying rainfall.

☐ **DOWNDRAFTS** are strong, gusty winds that rush down to the surface of the ground.

☐ **SPOT FIRES** occur when burning debris and embers that are blown ahead of the main fire land and start new fires.

☐ The **HEAD** of the fire is the main wall of flames that is advancing most quickly forward, usually with the wind.

☐ When firefighters are **WORKING FROM BEHIND,** they are at the sides or rear of the fire, not at its head.

YARNELL HILL, ARIZONA

FRIDAY, JUNE 28, 2013

On this day, a dry lightning strike started a fire in remote Yarnell Hill. By the next day, it had grown to about 100 acres; by early Sunday, it had reached more than 1,000 acres. Authorities called in the 20-man Granite Mountain Hotshot Team, all experts in fighting wildfires on difficult terrain. All day, the team fought the fire safely from behind. At about 3:30 P.M., a nearby thunderstorm produced winds in excess of 40 mph from a new direction. The fire quickly reversed course and came directly at the crew. Unable to escape in the mountainous terrain, 19 members of the team deployed their emergency shelters—one-person tents that reflect heat and provide breathable air for a short time in a fast-moving fire. Tragically, the shelters were no match for the intense fire, and the Hotshots perished. Only the lone lookout survived. This was the greatest loss for U.S. wildfire fighters in nearly 80 years.

PLANT
✻ a ✻
GROCERY
Garden!

Learn how to grow interesting
and unusual houseplants
from seeds and pits. Here are a few
fun and easy projects to try.

✻PEANUTS

Use fresh, unroasted peanuts. Avoid this project if you have an allergy to nuts (see page 128).

- Fill a wide, 4-inch-deep plastic container two-thirds full of moist potting soil.
- Shell four peanuts and place them on top of the soil, then cover with 1 inch of soil. Keep moist.
- Plants will sprout quickly.
- In a couple of months, small, yellow, pea-like flowers will develop along the lower part of the stem. After the flowers fade, short stems form, start to grow toward the ground, and then push themselves into the soil.
- Peanuts will be ready to harvest in about 6 months.

CITRUS

Most oranges, grapefruit, lemons, and tangerines contain seeds that can be used to sprout citrus plants.

- Soak the seeds in water overnight. If you are soaking seeds of different fruit, keep them separate.

- Nearly fill an 8- to 10-inch-diameter plant container (make sure that it has holes in the bottom) with moist potting soil. Plant each seed ½ inch deep in the soil: Push your index finger into the soil to the first knuckle. Put the seed into the hole and cover it up.

- Cover the pot with a plastic bag or piece of plastic wrap and put it in a warm spot. When the seeds start to grow in a few weeks, remove the plastic. Keep the pot in a warm, sunny window.

BEANS, PEAS, AND LENTILS

Before they're used in a homemade soup, save a few dried beans, peas, or lentils and bring them back to life.

- Soak the dried beans, peas, or lentils overnight in warm water. They look different, so you don't have to separate them.

- Fill an 8- to 10-inch-diameter pot (make sure that it has holes on the bottom) two-thirds full of moist potting soil.

- Place three seeds on the top of the soil and cover with ½ inch of soil. (Or use your finger as described for the citrus seeds.)

- Cover the pot with a plastic bag or plastic wrap and put in a warm spot. After the seeds sprout, remove the plastic.

- Put the pot in a warm, sunny window, and keep the soil evenly moist. Be prepared to tie the plants to a small stake as they grow.

IN THE GARDEN

❊PINEAPPLES

When it drizzles on a sunny day in Hawaii, locals call it "pineapple juice."

- Hold the pineapple's crown of leaves with one hand and its body with the other. Twist until the crown comes off the fruit.

- Peel off the crown's bottom leaves and discard them. The resulting stump will hold the roots. Let the crown dry out for 2 to 3 days.

- Put the stump into a glass of water on top of the refrigerator. Change the water regularly and keep it out of direct sun. Roots appear in a few weeks.

- Transplant the stump to a pot (make sure that it has holes in the bottom) with fast-draining potting soil and put in a sunny window. Keep moist.

- Repot the plant after 1 year has passed.

- After 2 more years, put the whole pot into a black plastic bag with a rotted apple cut in half. Put one half of the apple in the crown and one half in the soil. Seal the bag and set it aside for 2 weeks.

- Open the bag. If you see growth in the crown, remove the apple halves and put the plant where it will get lots of sun. If there is no growth, seal the bag for 2 more weeks.

- Flowers should appear 6 months after the first sign of growth.

❊MANGOES

India produces more than 50 percent of the world's mangoes. Fat from the seed is used to make soap. Some people are sensitive to the urushiol in the skin of mangoes. Avoid this project if you are susceptible to poison ivy.

- In the mango, there is a large, hairy pit. The seed is inside. Carefully, using a knife, scrape the excess flesh from the pit.

- With a dull knife (not a sharp knife; try a butter knife), gently pry open the pit and remove the seed.

❊AVOCADOS

The "alligator pear" is actually the berry of the avocado tree.

- Remove the pit from an avocado. Wash the pit and allow it to dry for 2 to 3 days.

- Stick three toothpicks into the pit's equator (or middle), equidistant apart and about ½ inch deep. Place the pit, with its fat base down, on the rim of a water glass, using the toothpicks to suspend it so that it doesn't fall into the glass. Add enough water to the glass to cover about an inch of the pit.

- Put the glass in a warm place out of direct sunlight. Add more water as needed. Roots and a stem should sprout in 2 to 6 weeks.

- When the stem is 6 to 7 inches long, cut it back to about 3 inches.

- When the roots are thick and the stem has grown out again, plant it in potting soil in an 8- to 10-inch-diameter pot, leaving the pit half-exposed.

- Set the pot in a sunny spot. Water the tree often, lightly, keeping the soil moist but not soaking wet. (Yellow leaves are a sign of too much water.) When the tree is about a foot high, cut it back to 6 inches so that new shoots will sprout.

- Soak it in water for at least 24 hours.

- Fill a small plastic bag with dampened peat moss or sphagnum (available at garden stores) or damp paper towels. Place the pit in the bag and surround it completely with peat moss. Close the bag halfway; leave it partly open to allow for air circulation. Put the bag in a sunny window.

- Check every day to make sure that the pit is not too dry or too wet. Moisten it, if necessary.

- When the roots are 4 inches long, transplant the seed to a pot that is at least 1 inch larger than the seed and nearly filled with potting soil. (Also make sure that the pot has holes on the bottom.) Water to keep it moist. Put it in a sunny spot and fertilize at least once in the summer.

Grow
a
Hideaway

Use fast-growing morning glories or pole beans to grow a teepee that can become a clubhouse for you and your friends or a secret hiding place where you can play or read a book.

YOU WILL NEED:

6 to 8 bamboo poles 6 feet long
sturdy twine or thin rope
scissors
gardening hand tools
peat moss or seed-starting mixture
1 package morning glory seeds or pole
   bean seeds
fertilizer (for beans)
1 package nasturtium seeds (optional;
   best with beans)

PICK A PLANT

Morning glories—so named because their flowers open in the morning—will grow 8 to 12 feet tall and 6 feet wide. There are more than 1,000 varieties, or types, that come with heart-shape leaves and flowers in solid and striped colors such as blue, pink, white, and yellow. The most common is bright blue with a white center.

Pole, or vining, beans will grow 6 to 9 feet tall. They come in dozens of varieties and can have pods that are green, yellow, a speckled combination of both, or even purple (these plants have violet flowers and purple beans that turn green when cooked). Scarlet runner beans have bright red flowers. Be sure that your beans are "pole beans." Bush beans are not vines and won't climb the poles.

Nasturtiums produce brilliant red, white, yellow, and orange flowers that would add color to your teepee.

MORNING GLORIES:

■ attract hummingbirds and butterflies

■ are related to sweet potatoes

■ have a scientific name *(Ipomoea)* that comes from the Greek words *ips* ("worm") and *homoios* ("like") because of their worm-like stem—you can almost see them grow!

■ have poisonous seeds

■ symbolize love and affection in the language of flowers

BEANS:

■ are so high in protein that some people eat them instead of meat

■ produce pods in 50 to 70 days, depending on the variety, making them one of the fastest-growing plants in the world

■ grow more (and more!) new pods as mature pods are picked

■ were used by ancient Greeks and Romans for voting: black to oppose, white to agree

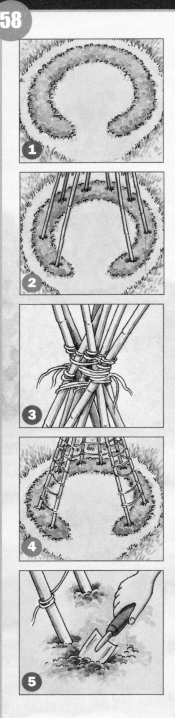

Plan to plant only after all danger of a frost has passed.

FIND A LOCATION

Ask an adult for help in finding a good place for your teepee and building it. The spot must get lots of sunshine and have good soil.

MAKE THE TEEPEE FRAME

1 Mark a 4- to 5-foot-diameter circle on the ground. The height of your teepee will depend on how large you make the circle. Leave yourself enough space to move around inside.

2 Mark a place for each pole about every 18 to 24 inches along the circle. Push each pole about 6 inches into the soil at a slight angle toward the middle. If the pole will not go into the ground, break up the soil or dig a small hole for each pole to get it deep enough.

3 Gather the poles together at the top where they meet. Wind the twine or rope tightly around the poles several times and tie it so that they will stand steady. Check that your teepee frame is sturdy and won't fall over. If it is weak, push the poles deeper into the ground.

4 Make a trellis for the plant vines to climb by tying twine around the teepee (leaving the entry open) and connecting it to the poles in four or five places each from top to bottom. The plants will climb the twine and make it shady inside.

PREPARE TO PLANT

5 Dig a small area around the outside base of each pole and loosen the soil.

6 Add a little peat moss or seed-starting mixture to the hole and work it into the soil. (Seeds start growing, or germinate, better in light, not heavy, soil.)

PLANT THE SEEDS

Soak the morning glory seeds in warm water overnight before you plant them. This will help the seed to break through its hard outer shell and germinate. Pole beans can be planted directly in the ground.

7 Plant two or three seeds in the loose soil around each pole. Set the morning glories ½ inch deep and the pole beans 1 inch deep. Cover them lightly with soil and pat gently.

8 In the soil between the poles, plant nasturtium seeds ½ to 1 inch deep, a couple of inches apart, and cover them with soil.

9 Water the plants deeply once a week or more often in hot, dry weather. Fertilize the beans according to the directions on the package.

10 As the plants grow and reach for the supports, gently guide them toward the poles and twine trellis.

Within a few weeks, your plants will be climbing the frame, brilliant flowers will be blooming, and your summer hideout will be complete.

Dried-Flow

By drying flowers,

**you can capture their color and enjoy them for weeks or longer.
Here's how to dry them and use them to decorate a candle.
(Allow about a week for flowers to dry.)**

YOU WILL NEED:
- **freshly picked flowers, such as pansies, violets, daisies, and geraniums**
- **fresh flower petals, such as those from flowers that have a large center, like coneflowers, sunflowers, roses, or peonies (optional)**
- **blades of grasses or clover leaves**
- **large, heavy books, such as atlases or dictionaries**
- **paper towels**

1. Pick flowers when they are in bloom in the afternoon or evening when the flowers are dry (not after they have been watered or are wet from rain). Select a few stems with leaves.

2. Open a book to the middle and place three paper towels on one page.

3. Arrange the flowers in a single layer on the paper towel so that they are not touching each other and will be completely inside the book when it is closed.

4. Place three more paper towels on top of the flowers and carefully close the book. Repeat these steps for flower petals and grasses, if using, in a separate book.

5. If necessary, place additional books (or other weights, such as canned goods) on top of the book.

6. In a week, open the book carefully. If the flowers are not completely dry, close the book for another day or two. If they are dry, lift out the paper towels with the flowers between them and set them aside.

er Delights

ASK, THEN PICK

Do not pick flowers from someone's garden without asking for permission—even if the owner of the garden is your mother or father.

Floral Candles

YOU WILL NEED:
- old newspaper
- decoupage glue (available in craft stores)
- small bowl
- paintbrush
- "pillar" candles, 2 to 4 inches in diameter and several inches tall
- dried flowers, leaves, blades of grass

1. Place several layers of newspaper on the work surface. Pour a small amount of glue into the bowl.

2. Using the paintbrush, dab a spot of glue the size of a flower on the candle. Gently press a flower in place. (Use small flowers on narrow candles and large flowers on wide ones.) Glue and press more dried flowers, leaves, and blades of grass onto the candle.

3. Brush the surface with glue to seal the flowers. Let it dry overnight.

GET GROWING!

Tried-and-true techniques for growing tasty treats

ROLL 'N' GROW

Some plant seeds—such as lettuce, radish, and carrot—are so tiny that they can easily fall from your fingers and get lost. A couple of weeks later, you might find the plants sprouting where you didn't want them. To make sure that your tiniest vegetable or flower seeds grow in straight rows where you want them, make a toilet paper seed strip first.

YOU WILL NEED:

toilet paper
2 tablespoons all-purpose flour
water

small paintbrush
ruler
seeds

1. Decide how long you want your row of plants to be.

2. Tear off enough toilet paper to fit in your row.

3. Put the flour into a small container or bowl and add a few drops of water. Stir to make a paste, adding more water, a drop or two at a time, as needed. (Make more paste, if you run out.)

4. Read your seed packet to see how far apart the seeds should be planted.

5. Using the paintbrush, make a row of paste "dots" on the toilet paper. Use a ruler as a guide to space the dots. You can make one row of dots down the middle of the toilet paper or make two rows about an inch from each edge. Add one or two seeds to each dot of paste.

6. When the paste is dry, carefully roll up the seed strip, bring it out to your garden, and lay it down, seed side up.

7. Read the seed packet to see how much dirt should cover the seeds and cover the seed strip.

8. Water the seeds with a gentle sprinkle now. Repeat as needed when the soil is dry.

The toilet paper will disintegrate in about a week. Your plants should sprout soon after that, perfectly spaced.

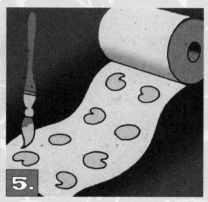

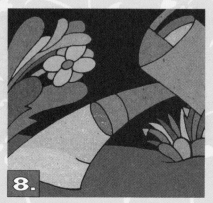

DO-IT-YOURSELF WATERING JUG

You can make a great watering "can" from an empty, clean, widemouth plastic juice jug or laundry detergent jug with a handle.

YOU WILL NEED:

WIDEMOUTH PLASTIC JUG, WITH TOP
HOUSEHOLD DRILL

1. Wash and rinse the jug thoroughly.

2. With an adult's help, drill holes in the widemouth top. This is the waterspout, so make the holes large enough that water will flow out easily but not so big that water will pour out.

3. With an adult's help, drill a slightly bigger air-release hole above the jug's handle.

4. Fill the jug with water, twist the top on it, and sprinkle your seeds and plants.

SACK-OF-SOIL GARDEN

The easiest garden that you can try is one that you grow in a bag of soil. A pot is not needed, but you must have a spot that is sunny most of the day. Garden soil can be purchased at a garden supply store.

Try lettuce, radish, or bean seeds; tomato, pepper, or strawberry plants; or pansies, zinnias, or marigolds.

YOU WILL NEED:

1 wheelbarrow or pull wagon (optional)
1 bag (20 lbs.) garden soil mixed with compost
seeds or plant seedlings

1. If you have a wheelbarrow, place the bag into it and lay the bag of soil flat. If not using a wheelbarrow, place the bag on the ground.

2. Poke a few holes in the top surface of the bag. These will allow water to drain out. Roll the bag over.

3. Cut a few holes in the new top surface for seeds or plants.

4. Read the seed packet and plant the seeds at the proper depth in the soil. If planting seedlings, create a space in the soil, set the plant into it, and gently tamp down the soil around it.

5. Water gently and as often as you would a garden bed.

6. Place the wheelbarrow in the sunlight for at least 6 hours a day. Do not allow a heavy rain to collect in the wheelbarrow, or the plants could drown.

FARMERS' MARKET FUN FACTS

CELERY

- leaves were worn by ancient Romans to cure headaches

- seeds were put into the shoes of medieval magicians who thought that they would enable them to fly

- fields in Oviedo, Florida, are said to be haunted by three children who died when their horse-drawn carriage overturned there centuries ago

POTATOES

- in dehydrated form, or flakes, have often been used as snow in films

- were the source of the starch that was an ingredient in the adhesive on the first lickable postage stamps

- peeled and kept in a pocket, can cure a toothache and eliminate a wart if rubbed on it, according to folklore

Corn

- ears all have an even number of rows

- husks were once used to stuff mattresses, including the one on which Abraham Lincoln was born

- popped and served with milk and maple sugar, was breakfast for New England colonists

PEAS

- have an unknown origin, but ancient Greeks enjoyed hot pea soup

- in the 1600s, were consumed by royalty before going to bed to avoid indigestion

- in poisoned form, were used by a British sympathizer in an attempt to kill George Washington, according to legend

- are traditionally planted on St. Patrick's Day, March 17

ON THE FARM

Cucumbers

■ being 96 percent water, were used to quench thirst centuries ago

■ sold from the family garden by 8-year-old Henry J. Heinz became his first business

■ in ancient China, were weighted with stones so that they would grow straight

EGGPLANT

■ got its name from early, small, oval, white varieties that resemble eggs

■ was made into a black dye by Chinese women in the 5th century to stain their teeth, which then shined like metal

■ was once thought to cause insanity if eaten, earning it the nickname "the mad apple"

CARROTS

■ have feathery green tops that were used to decorate women's hats and sleeves

■ were eaten on a stick by adults and children in the 1940s

■ could grow to be 2 feet long, measure 12 inches across at the top, and weigh as much as 4 pounds in the 1800s

TONGUE TWISTER

Can you say this five times fast?
Three blue beans in a blue bladder.
(A child's rattle was known as a "bladder.")

Beans

- were thought to cure toothaches and smallpox and to scare away ghosts when spat at them

- were eaten by Native Americans 600 years before the Pilgrims landed

RIDDLE WRANGLE

Knock, knock.
Who's there?
Lettuce.
Lettuce who?
Lettuce in and you'll find out.

LETTUCE

- was once believed to put people to sleep

- harvested by ancient Romans from the Greek island of Cos was first called *romaine*

- became a slang term for "money" because both are green

Peppers (Hot)

JUMP ROPE JIVE
Mabel, Mabel, set the table
And don't forget the red . . . hot . . . pepper!
(Begin counting jumps.)

- have "heat," or pungency, that comes from flavorless, odorless chemical compounds called capsaicinoids

- have "heat" that can be put out with yogurt, milk, or ice cream

- in jump rope, means turning the rope fast as jumpers compete to see who can make the most jumps during "red hot peppers"

ONIONS

- have crackly, paperlike skin known sometimes as the "tunic"

- that caused bad breath were called "skunk eggs" by cowboys

- have juice that at one time was believed to make hair grow if rubbed on a bald head

WEATHER FORECAST
Onion's skin very thin,
Mild winter coming in.
Onion's skin thick and tough,
Coming winter cold and rough.

ASPARAGUS

- can grow as much as 6 to 7 inches in 1 day

- contains an acid that makes some people's pee smell

- was so beloved by ancient Roman emperor Augustus that he built a fleet of ships to transport his harvest

SQUASHES

- of the hard-shell type are grown mainly in North America

- have a name that comes from the Massachusetts Native American word *askutasquash*, meaning "eaten raw"

- include pumpkins and other types, including the butternut, which Australians insist on calling the "butternut pumpkin"

Tomatoes

- are fruit, not vegetables, because they develop from flowers and have seeds

- 300 of the cherry variety have about the same number of calories as a chocolate ice cream cone

- have been shown to increase skin's ability to stave off UV-induced damage

The Farmer and the Rat

Centuries ago, farm families had major problems with rats that ate their grain. In the hope of ridding their property of rodents, some farmers wrote letters to the rats and placed the letters in the walls of their home or barn. This is the story of one such farmer and one smart rat.

With winter coming, Farmer John filled livestock bins with feed:
Oats for horses, corn for cows, and for spring crops, some seed.
He checked the stockpile every day. He hoped to make it last.
But then one day, too much was gone. Cried Farmer John aghast,
"What happened to my stores of feed? I'm sure I've used just some.
My livestock will run out of food before the snow has come!"

Right then a brown rat scurried by. He looked the well-fed sort.
As Farmer John yelled "Scat!" to him, he laughed a little snort.
"I'll drive you out, you thieving rat!" And then turned loose his dog.
Dog chased the rat, but Rat still laughed, "Why, thank you for the jog!"
The next day when the farmer checked again, the grain had dwindled.
And with the loss, the farmer found his anger was rekindled.

"A trap," John said, "of finest steel is what I need to set,
And bait it with some stinky cheese. I'll catch this robber yet."
He set the trap and left it where it could be found with ease
Unaware that Mister Rat had dairy allergies.
Rat did not even give a lick. He did not want to try it.
He'd lived a long and prosperous life upon his cheese-free diet.

🐀 "What should I do to stop that rat?" John asked his friend, Judge Sloan.
"I want that rat to go away and leave my grain alone."
"Then send a letter," said Judge Sloan, sounding quite judicial.
"A Notice of Eviction signed and sealed, to be official."
So John prepared the missive with unshakable conviction:
That rat would go once he received this Notice of Eviction.

🐀 "Dear Rat," wrote John, "I must protect the livestock in my care.
What's in my barn must go to them and you'll not have a share.
I am the landlord of this place, so heed the words I say.
You must vacate the premises before the break of day."
Rat found the notice, studied it, and then took out his pen.
And came up with a sly reply while winking at a hen.

🐀 "Dear Farmer," wrote the clever rat in round and perfect scrawl,
"I examined that fine note that you have nailed upon the wall.
Of all the farmers I have met, you're funniest, indeed,
Since every farmer ought to know a rodent can not read!"
It was signed along the bottom with the same neat *Rattus* scrawl:
"Please take care of Earth's creatures be they very great or small."

🐀 When John was doing chores, he found the note within the feed.
"He surely writes a fine hand for a rat who can not read."
He pondered Rat's short message, though, and then he just gave in.
"But I will only set aside one tiny little bin."
He posted notice number two: "Please take just what you need.
And share with my good cows and pigs the balance of the feed."

🐀 To his literary prowess, Mr. Rat never confessed.
But he only ate a small amount and he felt truly blessed.
And so at last a pact was reached; their differences surmountable.
As for the mice that just moved in, Rat couldn't be held accountable.

Amazing Inventions

GOT AN IDEA? THESE KIDS HAD ONE—AND IT CHANGED THEIR LIVES (AND MANY OF OURS, TOO)!

Hart Main

HE CAN AND HE DID

● In 2010, Hart Main's sister was selling candles for a school fund-raiser in Marysville, Ohio. To 13-year-old Hart, the candles were "really girlie scents." He suggested that the candles should have scents that men like, such as bacon, grass, sawdust, and leather. Hart meant it as just a joke, but his parents encouraged him to do something. As a result, he created Man-Cans, candles with the aroma of coffee, sawdust, dirt, grass, a new baseball mitt, bacon, and campfire. The Main family buys canned soup and donates it to community kitchens and homeless shelters, and these facilities return the clean, empty cans to Hart for use as candleholders.

Learn more at man-cans.com.

EVERYBODY LOVES EPSICLES!

● While growing up in Oakland, California, Frank Epperson had little idea that he would invent one of the most popular treats of all time. In 1905, when he was 11, he accidentally left a cup of flavored soda water with a stirring stick in it on his porch overnight. The next morning, Frank found the concoction frozen—and delicious! Eventually, in 1923, he patented his "frozen confection" and named it the "Epsicle." However, his children called it "Pop's 'sicle"—and that's how we know it today.

Jumping for Joy

● In 1930, 16-year-old George Nissen, a member of his high school's gymnastics and diving teams, wanted to practice some jumps. In his parents' garage in Cedar Rapids, Iowa, he stretched canvas over a rectangular steel frame and jumped on it.

Several years later, while in business school at the University of Iowa, he and his gymnastics coach improved the invention with nylon fabric. George and two friends started a traveling acrobatics troupe and used the "bouncing rig" in their act. While in the U.S. Midwest and Southwest, they learned the Spanish word for diving board, *trampolin.* George added an "e" and changed the name of the rig to "Trampoline," and he got a patent for it.

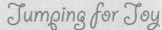

Pedal Power

● In 1998, while visiting a children's hospital, 6-year-old Spencer Whale from Pittsburgh, Pennsylvania, noticed that sick children who pedaled around in play vehicles were tethered to medical machines. Spencer designed a small pedal car and attached to it an intravenous (I.V.) pole, which holds a bag of fluid medicine that can drip slowly through a tube directly into a sick child. By using this, kids can play safely and have their medicine go with them. Many children's hospitals across the country now own KidKare cars and trucks.

My little WORLD

FOODWORLD

Jordan Casey

HE'S GOT GAME

● In 2009, when Jordan Casey of Waterford, Ireland, was 9, he enjoyed computer games so much that he bought a book to learn how to program. Then he made a Web site and blogged about games. Soon he was making his own games, and when he was 12, he started a company called Casey Games. Today, he continues to program, develops apps, has two companies, and speaks and consults around the world.

ALL WET

- In 1996, when Richie Stachowski, of Orinda, California, was 11, his family went to Hawaii. While snorkeling with his family, Richie wanted to shout out every time he saw a wildly colored fish—but a simple device for talking underwater did not exist. Richie began sketching designs and building prototypes of an underwater megaphone. In 1997, he patented and began selling Richie's Water Talkies, which allowed people to talk underwater from up to 15 feet away. A few years later he sold his company, but Richie's Water Talkies are still in stores today.

Something Up Her Sleeve

- In 1994, 10-year-old Kathryn Gregory was building a snow fort with her brother in New England, and snow got up in between her mittens and coat sleeves. This inspired her to create the first pair of wristies—a fingerless glove made of fleece that goes halfway up the arm under a coat, keeping wrists warm and dry, with or without mittens.

Today, wristies are worn by skiers, motorcyclists, musicians, runners, kids, and anyone who needs extra warmth and protection.

Learn more at wristies.com.

Kathryn Gregory

Abbey Fleck

No More Mess

● In 1991, 8-year-old Abbey Fleck was cooking bacon with her dad in St. Paul, Minnesota. They ran out of paper towels, so he put the bacon on newspaper to drain. Abbey thought that if they could create a dish to catch the grease, they would not need paper towels or newspaper. She and her father designed a square, 1-inch-deep, microwave-safe skillet, with three supports in the center. Bacon is draped over the supports and, as it cooks, fat drips into the dish. The Makin' Bacon cooker is now sold in stores across the country.

Learn more at makinbacon.com.

NOW 'EAR THIS

● In 1873, in Farmington, Maine, 15-year-old Chester Greenwood was testing out a pair of ice skates but was getting frustrated because his ears were so cold. He made two round loops out of wire and asked his grandmother to sew fur on them. After connecting them with a steel headband, he eventually got a patent for Greenwood's Champion Ear Protectors—otherwise known as earmuffs.

KIDS' GREAT FINDS

The next time your PARENTS send you OUTSIDE for some fresh air, keep your EYES open. Search the SKIES and the GROUND: You never know what you may DISCOVER.

A SUPER SIBLING RIVALRY

When Kathryn Gray of Fredericton, New Brunswick, heard that the youngest person to discover a supernova, Caroline Moore of Warwick, New York, had been 14 at the time, she decided that she wanted to beat this record.

On January 2, 2011, the 10-year-old accomplished her goal. She was guided by her father, Paul, an amateur astronomer, who taught her to use a computer program to compare images of the same view of the night sky taken at different times. (These images were sent to her father from the telescope of another astronomer.) Her father told her that a flash of light where none had been before might be a supernova. While carefully examining the fourth image in a set of 52, Kathryn asked, "Is this one?" It was!

Her discovery, now called Supernova 2010lt, is about 240 million light-years away from Earth.

Almost 3 years later, on October 30, 2013, Kathryn's brother Nathan broke his sister's record. Just 9 days after his 10th birthday, while he was studying images of the sky, Nathan spotted supernova 2013hc, which is 600 million years old. With this find, he became the star, inheriting his sister's title of youngest person to discover a supernova. He was 33 days younger than Kathryn was when she made her discovery, and he had been trying to beat his sister's record for 8 months.

Paul Gray is also a supernovae discoverer. The first time was in 1995, when he was 22 years old, making him the then-youngest person to discover one. He has discovered six in all: SN1995F, 2005b, 2005ea, 2007R, 2007ac, and 2007ad.

WHAT'S A SUPERNOVA?

A supernova is an explosion caused by a star at the end of its life. These explosions briefly can be brighter than entire galaxies, sending out more energy than our Sun in its lifetime. Supernovae are some of the most energy-filled explosions in nature.

A GOOD EYE IN BADLANDS

In May 2010, 7-year-old Kylie Ferguson and her family from Sharpsburg, Georgia, visited South Dakota's Badlands National Park, one of the world's best hunting grounds for fossils. In addition to saber-toothed cats, mammals such as camels, rhinos, and three-toed horses once roamed the area.

Like many young visitors, Kylie took part in the Junior Ranger Program, which encourages kids to explore the National Parks. Unlike most kids, Kylie made a major fossil find when she noticed something interesting in some limestone near the park's visitor center.

After she reported her discovery to rangers, paleontologists first thought that the bones belonged to an extinct animal similar to a sheep. However, heavy rains later exposed more of the bones, and scientists concluded that Kylie had instead found the rare, well-preserved fossil of a saber-toothed cat about 32 million years old.

Kylie's fossil has been excavated and added to the park's museum collection. Anytime Kylie visits Badlands National Park, she can proudly point out the area where she made her discovery, now known as the Saber Site.

FROM GROSS TO "GOLDEN"

As he walked the beach in England with his father in 2012, 8-year-old Charlie Naysmith poked at a clump of seaweed. He spotted a light gray rock with an interesting texture and decided to keep it.

Once home, Charlie and his dad tried to identify the rock and soon realized that this wasn't really a rock. Instead, Charlie had found a treasure known as ambergris (AM-bur-griss)—worth about $65,000. One reason that ambergris is so valuable is that it's hard to find.

The specimen had come from a sperm whale. Whales eat a lot of squid, which have pointed beaks that are hard to digest. Sperm whales sometimes produce ambergris, a greasy substance that coats the squid beaks and protects the whale's intestines after it swallows a squid or a cuttlefish, which also has a horny beak.

Ambergris has been described as "whale vomit," but scientists now believe that the substance leaves through the back end of these large mammals. (No one really knows where it comes out, because no one has witnessed the process.) Ambergris leaves whales in clumps, some weighing hundreds of pounds. Once in the ocean, this black, stinky stuff floats and hardens and changes color. It eventually breaks into smaller pieces.

The odor of fresh ambergris has been compared to that of an old wooden church or seaweed. After ambergris hardens in the ocean, it smells much better.

Also called "floating gold," ambergris has been used for many things for thousands of years, including incense and medicine as well as perfume. American perfumes don't contain it anymore because sperm whales are endangered.

Charlie is a nature lover who says that he hopes to sell his treasure and use the money to build an animal preserve.

PERSISTENCE THAT PAID OFF

"Not again," Dr. Carl Agee thought when 13-year-old Jansen Lyons showed him a 2-pound rock. Dr. Agee is a meteorite expert, and people often ask him to examine their finds. Usually, these specimens are just ordinary Earth rocks or, as Dr. Agee calls them, "meteor-wrongs."

In 2012, Jansen dropped by Dr. Agee's office at the University of New Mexico's Institute of Meteoritics in Albuquerque. The boy became a meteor hunter after reading a book on the subject in 2008. His grandfather made him several metal detectors (95 percent of meteorites are made of iron), and Jansen used them to search many local areas (after getting permission from property owners).

In September 2011 in his hometown of Rio Rancho, New Mexico, Jansen found an interesting rock. After comparing it with photographs of meteorites, he believed that he had something.

In June, Jansen and his mother visited Dr. Agee, who took a sample of Jansen's discovery for closer examination. By the time that Jansen had returned home, Dr. Agee had called to say that this was indeed a meteorite. The chunk had probably been resting on Earth for 10,000 years.

Jansen named his discovery "Rio Rancho," and the Meteorological Society officially approved the find.

WHAT'S A METEORITE?

Meteorites are pieces of asteroids (and sometimes comets) that fall from space to Earth. A few have even been pieces of Mars and the Moon. So far, about 40,000 have been found and cataloged, and many of these are quite valuable. Meteorites are often black, and they're easiest to spot in dry, desertlike conditions.

A FORTUNE AT HIS FEET

Instead of going to church services one Sunday morning in 1799, 12-year-old Conrad Reed went fishing in Meadow Creek, near his home in Mecklenburg County, North Carolina. Before long, he spotted an intriguing yellow rock. He lugged it home and, for a while, the 17-pound stone served as a useful doorstop.

Eventually, Conrad's father John asked a local silversmith to identify the mass, but the man could not. In 1802, another jeweler informed John that the rock was gold and that he would like to buy it. They agreed on what John felt was a "big" price: $3.50.

John soon smartened up and, legend has it, returned to the jeweler and got about $1,000 more. Then he and his family headed back to Meadow Creek, where John partnered with his brother-in-law and a wealthy landowner in their search for more gold. Before long, one of the landowner's slaves had found a 28-pound specimen worth more than $6,600.

Conrad's Sunday diversion, the first documented gold strike in the United States, made his family wealthy. North Carolina led the nation in gold production until the California gold rush began in 1848. Today, the Reed Gold Mine remains open for tours.

From left:
Burrito Boyz
Nick Peeleman,
Justin McDonald,
Alec Johnson,
Luke Trolinger,
Joe Skvarna,
Julian Wahl,
and Cole Smith

IN 2010, when Alec Johnson of San Diego, California, was 12, he wrote his Christmas list and showed it to his parents. On it were a lot of high-priced electronic items. His parents encouraged him to think about other people and suggested that he volunteer in the community. "At first I thought my parents just wanted to teach me a lesson. It was only supposed to be a one-time experience," says Alec.

ALEC DECIDED TO MAKE breakfast burritos to serve to the homeless. The first Sunday, he and his dad, plus his best friend, Luke, made 54 egg-and-cheese burritos in the Johnsons' kitchen and delivered them, with 54 bottles of water, to homeless people in San Diego.

SOON, THE "BURRITO BOYZ" were making 120 burritos per week and needed a larger kitchen. A local restaurant donated the use of theirs.

MAKING A
DIFFERENCE
IN MANY
DIFFERENT
WAYS

GIVING
KIDS

SINCE THAT FIRST SUNDAY in November 2010, six of Alec's friends have joined him. One meal of 620 burritos used 1,344 eggs, 90 pounds of potatoes, 35 pounds of cheese, and 620 tortillas. The eggs are donated (as well as bagels, which are also given out), and an annual fund-raiser raises about $10,000 a year that is used to buy potatoes, cheese, and tortillas.

THE BURRITO BOYZ HAVE GROWN to include more than 50 volunteers, including Girl Scouts and kids who are "in training" to take over when Alec and his friends head to college. By April 2015, he and his Boyz had made and served 93,081 burritos to the homeless in San Diego across 232 Sundays in a row. Alec says that the experience has taught him not only how he can make a difference, but also, more importantly: "Whatever you put your mind to, try your hardest. Just go out and do it."

LEARN MORE AT BURRITOBOYZ.ORG.

ONE DAY, JESSICA CARSCADDEN'S mother asked her to clean her room. Jessica started by getting rid of some of her stuffed animals. She gave them to local firefighters and policemen to keep in their trucks and cars to give to children they met when they were called to a fire or a car accident. "A stuffed animal helps to turn a scary memory into a less scary memory," says Jessica.

AT FIRST, JESSICA DONATED only her own stuffed animals. Now, schools and Girl Scout troops sponsor "We Care Bears" drives to donate stuffed animals. So far, Jessica has collected about 10,000 stuffed animals and distributed them to emergency response vehicles throughout southern California and Las Vegas, Nevada.

ALL STUFFED ANIMALS are accepted, although new or very gently used are ideal. Jessica says, "I never say no to any stuffed animal. Maybe a dirty old stuffed animal is that child's favorite, and giving it away is a big act of love. We accept them just as if they were the best stuffed animal in the world.

"I WANT ALL KIDS TO KNOW that they are never too small to do amazing things. When I was born, I had a physical problem with my mouth. I went to live in an orphanage. I was adopted when I was 5, and I've had five big surgeries. You don't have to have a big project to make a difference. Even just saying something nice to one new person every day can make the world better."

LEARN MORE AT WECAREBEARS.COM.

MYLES ECKERT of Waterville, Ohio, was only 5 weeks old when his soldier father died in action. Myles has said that every time he sees a soldier, he is reminded of his dad.

WHEN HE WAS 9 in February 2014, Myles and his family were going into a restaurant in Maumee, Ohio. In the parking lot, he found a $20 bill. Myles and his sister, Marlee, decided to give the $20 to a soldier who was eating there. Myles wrote a note: "Dear Soldier—my dad was a soldier. He's in heaven now. I found this $20 in the parking lot when we got here. We like to pay it forward in my family. It's your lucky day! Thank you for your service. Myles Eckert, a Gold Star kid."

SOON, LOCAL NEWSPAPERS and television stations heard about Myles's generosity. He was even on national television. People began sending money to Myles and his family to help families of fallen soldiers. Myles's mom, Tiffany, arranged to have the donations managed through Snowball Express, an organization that helps veterans and their families, as well as the American Legion and Gold Star kids, which grant scholarships to children who have a parent who has fallen in the line of duty. Myles says that he likes being a part of this effort because it's not selfish and it's like he is paying it forward.

THAT'S NOT ALL. When a restaurant offered to give an ice cream party for the kids at Myles's school, Myles asked that they do it at a school that has many children with learning disabilities. Myles also has a learning disability, but the experience with this project has helped him. "At school, I used to be bullied. Now kids are asking to be my friend," he says.

LEARN MORE AT SNOWBALLEXPRESS.ORG.

BOWS AND BALLCAPS

HANNAH GRUBBS HAS been bald her whole life because of a disease called *Alopecia areata,* which causes hair loss. When she was very young, people often thought that she had cancer and would go out of their way to be nice to her; one friend once gave her a soft, felt hairband with a bow—which would later give Hannah an idea.

AT THE AGE OF 9, Hannah decided that she wanted to repay all of the kindness that she had received and do something for children who had cancer or Alopecia by giving them a bow or ball cap to wear. Her Bows & Ballcaps project began with a $250 donation that she used for supplies.

NOW, A FRIEND IN Hannah's hometown of Hendersonville, Tennessee, makes the bows, and the company Lids donates the ball caps. Hannah distributes the bows and ball caps to local children's hospitals, including 500 bows and ball caps to the Vanderbilt Children's Hospital in Nashville.

HANNAH ALSO MAKES care packages for children, adding bracelets, games, puzzles, lip gloss, and small stuffed animals. "If possible," she says, "I like to personalize them, and I base items in the package on their age and interests."

HANNAH TRIES TO give out 50 care packages each month. Her goals are simple: "I want the kids to have a happy face. I want them to know that someone cares, and the care packages deliver that message. I want people to know that everyone can make a difference, even if they are only 10. If you are passionate about something, you can make a difference. If someone is hurt, you can help them. You don't need to start a charity."

LEARN MORE AT BOWSANDBALLCAPS.COM.

WHEN MILO CRESS WAS 9, he realized that every time he ordered a drink in a restaurant, it came with a plastic straw, and most of the time, he didn't use the straw.

HE HAS SINCE LEARNED that about 500 million straws are used every day in the United States and that discarded straws are one of the most common types of trash that washes up on beaches. Many animals, including birds and turtles, die or are injured from eating plastic, and Milo realized that he could do something about this.

HE ASKED HIS FRIENDS to go without a straw when they were in a restaurant and encouraged the staff at a local restaurant to ask customers if they wanted a straw before giving one to them. From there, his "Be Straw Free" project grew.

MILO ASKED POLITICIANS to help spread his message. He visited the then-mayor of his hometown of Burlington, Vermont, who issued a proclamation supporting Milo's project. He contacted the mayors of Manly, Australia, and Denver, Colorado, and the governor of Colorado, who proclaimed a Colorado Straw Free Day. Later, Milo was invited to Washington, D.C., by the Vermont congressional delegation, where he presented his ideas to U.S. senators and congressmen.

MILO NOW SPEAKS AT conferences and schools around the world as part of his "Let's Create the Future" international speaking tour. He hopes that he is an example for other kids who want to make a difference. He says, "My project helps the environment and it helps kids."

LEARN MORE AT ECOCYCLE.ORG/BESTRAWFREE.

WEEVIL

GO BUGGY!

A CREEPY-CRAWLY FIELD GUIDE

GRASSHOPPER

TARANTULA

We live amid untold numbers of tiny creatures. In fact, scientists know of about 1 million different types of insects alone—and this doesn't include spiders, which aren't "insects"! Explore this wondrous world with these fun facts and activities.

UP CLOSE

■ Insects have three parts to their body and six legs.

■ Spiders have two body parts and eight legs.

■ "Bugs" technically are a type of insect with a beaklike mouth used to suck juice from plants, but many folks refer to all insects and spiders as "bugs."

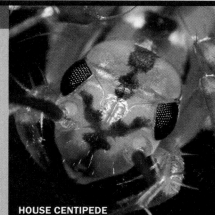

HOUSE CENTIPEDE

BUILD A BUG HOTEL

Befriend some bugs. Build them a home. Do it on a flat spot, in sun or shade—but first get your parents' approval on the place!

■ Stack bricks, pots, and boards as shown below. Between layers, insert twigs, branches, pinecones, old flowerpot pieces, and dried leaves.

■ Treat your little guests to paper towel or toilet paper rolls filled with things like cardboard and straws.

EARWIG

CADDIS FLIES

Caddis flies look like small moths with long antennae. Long, silky hair covers most of their body and wings. Young caddis flies live underwater. Soon after birth, they build a protective tubular case out of twigs, leaves, shells, and gravel, gluing them together with a sticky substance from their mouths. Babies can stick their head in and out of it.

Eventually the caddis fly pupates, or rests, for 2 weeks. Then it pushes out of its case, finds its way to the surface of the water, and flies away, looking like a moth.

WHERE THEY LIVE

■ near ponds and rivers around the world; they are attracted to light at night

WHAT THEY EAT

■ algae, water fleas, aquatic worms, leaves, and things on the stream or pond bottom (eaten by juveniles; adults, who live for only a month, don't eat)

DID YOU KNOW?

■ Fish love to munch on caddis flies! This is why these insects are often used as models for the artificial flies that fishermen make and use.

CENTIPEDES

Centipedes are sometimes called 100-legged worms, even though they can have from 15 to 177 pairs of legs. They have poison glands inside their claws—useful for paralyzing things that they like to eat, such as small insects. Never fear! Centipede jaws are not usually strong enough to break through human skin, and even if they do, the pain is no worse than that of a bee sting. These bugs are not insects; they're more closely related to lobsters and shrimp.

WHERE THEY LIVE

■ dark, damp places in homes (basements, closets, and bathrooms) and gardens (under rocks, sticks, or leaves) throughout North America and around the world

WHAT THEY EAT

■ a variety of insects

DID YOU KNOW?

■ Centipedes always have an odd number of pairs of legs.
■ The Peruvian giant centipede can grow up to a foot long. It likes to hang on the ceiling of a cave, pluck a bat right out of the air, and eat it.

EARWIGS

Earwigs are dark, reddish brown bugs with flat, long bodies and two pairs of wings. They're known for their pincers, called forceps. These insects are nocturnal, or active at night.

WHERE THEY LIVE

■ damp, dark places such as in mulch, under flowerpots, and in basements

WHAT THEY EAT

■ a variety of plant and animal matter, such as leaves or dead insects

DID YOU KNOW?

■ There's a superstition that earwigs crawl into people's ears at night and then eat their brains. False! Earwigs don't hurt people, but they may pinch.

COCKROACHES

Cockroaches are nocturnal, or active at night. As cockroaches move about the house, they can spread germs to food, as well as to things like plates and forks. The result: People who touch or eat these things can get food poisoning or diarrhea.

WHERE THEY LIVE

■ small cracks and crevices in homes, hospitals, restaurants, and other buildings, especially where food is present; also forests and caves

WHAT THEY EAT

■ almost anything—food scraps, soap, glue, and even electronics and wiring! Some can survive for weeks without a meal.

DID YOU KNOW?

■ One woman in China has a breeding population of about 100,000 cockroaches. She lives nearby but checks the bugs each day and says that she treats them "like her children." She sells them to a drug company that uses the roaches in certain Asian medicines.

GRASSHOPPERS

Grasshoppers are common insects that can not only fly but also jump great distances on their powerful hind legs. They make music by rubbing these back legs against their forewings.

WHERE THEY LIVE

■ gardens, fields, forests, and deserts around the world

WHAT THEY EAT

■ Grasshoppers eat plants, and swarms of them can damage crops. Locusts are a particularly damaging type of grasshopper.

DID YOU KNOW?

■ At the end of May 2014, so many grasshoppers swarmed around Albuquerque, New Mexico, that the insects showed up on radar!
■ In many parts of the world, people eat grasshoppers. They're a great source of protein. Chocolate-covered grasshoppers, anyone?

TRY THIS!

■ Some grasshoppers spit out a brown substance as defense if they're handled. If you catch a grasshopper, try gently rubbing its mouth near a white piece of paper—you might get spit at!

LADYBUGS

Not only are ladybugs cute, but also they're a big help to farmers. These beetles, also called ladybirds and ladybird beetles, help to protect crops by eating lots of plant-eating insects. Like butterflies, ladybugs go through a complete metamorphosis, starting out as caterpillar-like larvae.

WHERE THEY LIVE

■ in winter, under logs or leaves or in warm places, often inside homes, especially in mild climates; in spring, around windows, trying to get outside, or in forests, fields, and gardens

WHAT THEY EAT

■ other insects, such as aphids, and insect eggs

DID YOU KNOW?

■ Ladybugs' bright colors remind predators to watch out! When threatened, a ladybug may play dead while secreting a bad-tasting substance to protect itself.
■ Many people believe that ladybugs are good luck.

SPIDERS

About 40,000 different species of spiders are known. Spiders are classified as arthropods. They catch food in their silken webs. Spider blood is pale blue in color.

WHERE THEY LIVE

■ from deserts to wetlands, and on every continent except Antarctica

WHAT THEY EAT

■ insects; a few types of spiders are large enough to eat small birds or mice

DID YOU KNOW?

■ The Moroccan flic-flac spider, recently discovered in a desert of Morocco, looks like a gymnast doing somersaults when it needs to make a quick escape.
■ Many people have arachnophobia (fear of spiders).

TRY THIS!

1. Find an empty spider web.
2. Gently sprinkle talcum powder over the web.
3. With an adult's help, spray hair spray on a piece of black construction paper. While the paper is still wet, move the paper onto the spider web so that it sticks.
4. Remove the paper. You can see one spider's work of art traced in talcum powder.

STINKBUGS

Stinkbugs do not smell good. When frightened, they release an odor from their glands that smells like stinky socks. If you touch one, hold your nose! These oval- and shield-shape bugs can also fly. Like ladybugs, stinkbugs often invade homes in search of winter warmth.

HABITAT

■ Different types are found in many states (they have no natural predators in North America). The brown marmorated stinkbug is common in Asia and was first spotted in North America in Allentown, Pennsylvania, in 1998.

WHAT THEY EAT

■ plants and crops, sometimes other insects

DID YOU KNOW?

■ A National Wildlife Federation scientist in Maryland named Doug Inkley found 56,205 stinkbugs in his house and garden one year. They were everywhere, sometimes even in his food! Inkley vacuumed up the bugs and sent them off to be studied.

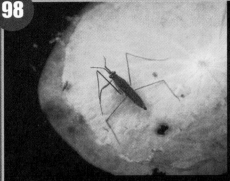

WATER STRIDERS

Water striders, also called pond skaters or skimmers, look like big mosquitoes with six long legs that seem to run or skate across the surface of the water. Tiny water-resistant hairs on their legs help them stay afloat.

WHERE THEY LIVE

■ the surfaces of ponds, marshes, and quiet streams

WHAT THEY EAT

■ living and dead insects, such as mosquitoes and dragonflies

DID YOU KNOW?

■ Water striders' short front legs are used for capturing other insects. The long middle legs help the insect move across the water. The long back legs are used for steering.

WEEVILS

Weevils are a type of beetle, usually a dark, oval-shape insect. Over 1,000 species in North America feed on and spoil crops and stored grains, such as wheat, and are named for the things that they eat. There are rose weevils, rice weevils, bean weevils, and wheat weevils. Boll weevils are famous for damaging cotton plants.

WHERE THEY LIVE

■ usually fields, gardens, and orchards

WHAT THEY EAT

■ plants and stored foods, such as grains and nuts

DID YOU KNOW?

■ Boll weevils came to the United States from Mexico in the 1890s and remained a terrible problem for cotton farmers for nearly 100 years. Most U.S. cotton-growing states are now boll weevil–free.

Bugged About Nutrition?

Around the world, mostly outside of North America, more than 2 billion people consume insects for breakfast, lunch, and/or dinner. They can choose from a wide variety—some 1,900 species are edible. Bugs are efficient to raise: Compared with beef and other animals, insects take up less space and can be fed less, and they have less impact on the environment. Best of all, for people, insects are highly nutritious, as shown below. Beetle burger, anyone?

Nutritional Makeup of Various Insects per 100 Grams*

INSECT	PROTEIN (g)	FAT (g)	CARBS**(g)	CALCIUM (mg)	IRON (mg)
Giant water beetle	19.8	8.3	2.1	43.5	13.6
Red ant	13.9	3.5	2.9	47.8	5.7
Silkworm pupa	9.6	5.6	2.3	41.7	1.8
Dung beetle	17.2	4.3	0.2	30.9	7.7
Cricket	12.9	5.5	5.1	75.8	9.5
Small grasshopper	20.6	6.1	3.9	35.2	5.0
Large grasshopper	14.3	3.3	2.2	27.5	3.0
June beetle	13.4	1.4	2.9	22.6	6.0
Termite	14.2	–	–	–	35.5
Weevil	6.7	–	–	–	13.1
COMPARED WITH:					
Beef (lean ground)	27.4	–	–	–	3.5
Fish (broiled cod)	28.5	–	–	–	1.0

g = grams; mg = milligrams; *about 3.5 ounces; **carbohydrates

–courtesy Department of Entomology, Iowa State University

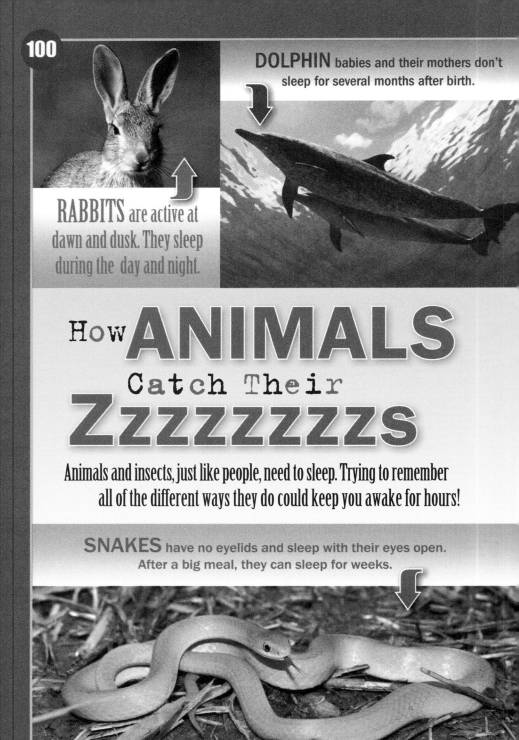

DOLPHIN babies and their mothers don't sleep for several months after birth.

RABBITS are active at dawn and dusk. They sleep during the day and night.

How **ANIMALS** Catch Their **Zzzzzzzzz**

Animals and insects, just like people, need to sleep. Trying to remember all of the different ways they do could keep you awake for hours!

SNAKES have no eyelids and sleep with their eyes open. After a big meal, they can sleep for weeks.

GIRAFFES take 5-minute naps throughout the day, for a total of about 30 minutes of sleep every 24 hours.

BROWN BATS

sleep for about 19 hours a day upside down. They can fly away more easily from this position.

DESERT SNAILS can sleep for up to 3 years.

WORKER FIRE ANTS take more than 250 naps every day, each lasting about 1 minute, 6 seconds.

KOALAS sleep in eucalyptus trees for 18 to 22 hours a day.

ALBATROSSES lock their wings and sleep while flying.

SEALS can sleep underwater or on land. When they are underwater, only half of their brain sleeps at a time; the other half stays awake.

PIGS prefer to sleep nose-to-nose with other pigs.

When **WALRUSES** sleep, they inflate their body with up to 13 gallons of air, allowing them to bob in the water. A walrus can swim without sleep for up to 3 days.

CROCODILES sleep with their mouths open. This aids in keeping them cool.

MALLARD DUCKS
sleep in rows while floating on water. The ducks on the ends of the row keep one eye open to watch for predators.

POLAR BEARS sleep in beds dug in the lee (out of the wind) side of a ridge, even through blizzards. Snow that piles up on top of them provides an insulating blanket.

SEA OTTERS sleep holding each other's paws, which helps to keep them from separating from their raft, or group. Sometimes they grab on to kelp with their tails so that they don't float away.

Many **BIRDS** can sleep with one eye open and half of their brain awake, while the other eye is closed and the other half of their brain is asleep. This enables them to keep an eye on predators.

OSTRICHES sleep lightly—sitting down—for 7 to 8 hours per night. They lie down for about 9 minutes of deep sleep.

BEWARE OF THE BEAR!

North American black bears are common in forests across the continent. They are different from grizzly bears, and they are not always black! Some are brown, cinnamon, blond, or even creamy white. Some have a patch of white fur on their chest.

Q:
What color are
bears' socks?
A:
They don't wear
socks. They
have bear feet!

Black bears eat mostly fruit, nuts, roots, insects, fish, and some small animals. When there is plenty of food in a bear's territory, it will share with other bears; if there is not enough food, it will chase off others.

A black bear marks its territory by rubbing its back against a tree or clawing it. Also, it urinates or makes sunken footprints along the boundary line. Other bears smell these markings and know that the territory is taken.

During the winter, bears hibernate in a den— a large hole in the ground, a cave, or a hollow log or tree. When hibernating, they sleep for up to 7 months. Their heart rate drops from 40 beats per minute to 8 to 19. They do not eat or drink.

When one bear greets another that it has not seen in a while, the two stand nose to nose, with their mouths open. These bears identify each other by the smell of their breath! To show friendship, sometimes bears wrestle.

BLACK BEAR OR GRIZZLY?

Black bears have . . .
- no front shoulder hump
- low shoulders, high rump
- short, curved claws
- paw prints with short claws, separate toes

Grizzly bears have . . .
- a hump of muscle above the front shoulders
- high shoulders, low rump
- long claws
- large, broad paw prints with long claws, close toes

DID YOU KNOW?

- *Ursus americanus* is the black bear's scientific name.
- Ursa and Ursus mean "bear" in Latin.
- Ursa Major ("Great Bear") and Ursa Minor ("Smaller Bear") are constellations that contain the asterisms (groups of stars) known as the Big Dipper and Little Dipper, respectively.

Bear cubs are born in January or February, while their mother is hibernating in her den. Cubs are born hairless and blind (and will have poor eyesight all their lives) and weigh less than 1 pound (yet can grow to 500 pounds or more). They stay with their mother for 1½ years or until they can take care of themselves. Papa bears leave before cubs are born and do not help to raise them.

Sometimes one bear will adopt another's cub, if the mother is unable to take care of it. If you see a bear cub alone, back away, being careful not to frighten it. Its mother, real or adoptive, is probably nearby, and she may think that you will harm it.

A mother bear usually sends small cubs up a tree to keep them safe while she is away looking for food. When food arrives, cubs may fight fiercely over it. When the cubs grow older, they hunt for food with their mother.

To hide from danger, black bears take cover behind rocks, bushes, logs and trees, and may even climb a tree. Small bears go out on a limb to get away from larger bears. Sometimes bears sleep in trees.

Black bears are fast runners (think of a racehorse) and excellent swimmers. Plus, their powerful sense of smell enables them to detect the aroma of food from long distances. They are also smart, with good memories. These are all good reasons to . . .

■ **Never feed bears. Do not leave food, garbage, birdseed, or pet food outside. It will attract bears, and once they have eaten once, they will return another time looking for more.**

■ **Never keep food in a tent. Outdoors, store food in bear-proof containers or, better yet, a closed and locked vehicle.**

■ **Avoid strong-smelling food— such as tuna sandwiches—when hiking or camping.**

Most bears try to avoid people; you should try to avoid bears. When walking through the woods (never alone!), make noises— like clapping, whistling, or talking—or wear bells on your shoes. This will scare away a bear, if it hears you coming.

If you do meet up with a bear, do not run or play dead. They are extremely unpredictable! Speak softly to it, avoid eye contact, and back away until you are out of sight or more than 25 feet away, then walk away. Do not throw anything, yell, scream, or wave your arms: This could make a bear angry or scared enough to attack.

TRACKER'S

BEAVER

HABITAT: Wetlands with trees—birch, willow, cottonwood, and aspen, in particular (for building material and food)

WEIGHT: Up to 60 pounds; the largest rodent in North America

LENGTH: 25 to 31 inches

DIET: Vegetarian; trees (the bark, not the wood), pond lilies, and other aquatic vegetation

TERRITORY: Throughout the United States, except the arid Southwest, southern Florida, and Hawaii; Canada

EASTERN CHIPMUNK

HABITAT: Deciduous forests, fallen logs, suburban and rural yards, city parks

WEIGHT: 3 to 6 ounces

LENGTH: 8 to 11 inches, including a 3- to 4-inch tail

DIET: Berries, grain, insects, nuts, seeds, slugs, small snakes, snails, worms

TERRITORY: Eastern and central United States; eastern Canada

MOOSE

HABITAT: Recently burned areas with willow and birch shrubs; dense forests; timberline plateaus; riversides

WEIGHT: Males, 1,200 to 1,600 pounds; females, 800 to 1,300 pounds

HEIGHT: 76 inches at shoulder, on average

DIET: Willow, cottonwood, fir trees; aquatic plants

TERRITORY: Northern United States; Canada

SNOWSHOE HARE

HABITAT: Forests, fields, riversides, swamps

WEIGHT: 2 to 4 pounds, on average

HEIGHT: 12 to 18 inches

DIET: Grass, clover, dandelions, raspberry and blackberry shoots, twigs, woody plants

TERRITORY: Northern United States; most of Canada

GUIDE

Off for a walk in the woods? Keep an eye out for signs of these woodland creatures.

COMMON RACCOON

HABITAT: Woodlands, grasslands, farmland, suburbs—especially if water is nearby

WEIGHT: Males, 15 to 30 pounds; females, 10 to 20 pounds

LENGTH: 26 to 42 inches, including an 8- to 14-inch tail

DIET: Berries, birds' eggs, cat food, corn, fish, frogs, insects, mice, nuts, salamanders, shellfish, garbage

TERRITORY: Throughout North America

STRIPED SKUNK

HABITAT: Woodlands, grasslands, farmland, suburbs

WEIGHT: Males, 3 to11 pounds; females, 2 to 8 pounds

LENGTH: 21 to 30 inches, including a 7- to 15-inch tail

DIET: Mice, shrews, eggs, grubs and other forms of insects, nuts, fruit, garbage

TERRITORY: Throughout the United States, except the arid Southwest; southern Canada

RED SQUIRREL

HABITAT: Coniferous and deciduous forests; wooded parks

WEIGHT: 8 to 12 ounces

LENGTH: 11 to 14 inches, including a 4- to 5-inch tail

DIET: Berries, birds' eggs, fruit, mushrooms and other fungi, nuts, seeds

TERRITORY: Northern United States; Rocky Mountains south to Arizona and New Mexico; Canada

GRAY WOLF

HABITAT: Forests, deserts, plains, mountains, tundra

WEIGHT: Males, 85 to 115 pounds; females, 50 to 100 pounds

HEIGHT: 26 to 32 inches at shoulder

DIET: Deer, elk, caribou, bison, cattle, sheep, beavers, rabbits, rodents, grass, nuts, berries

TERRITORY: North central, northwestern (including Alaska) and southwestern United States; Canada

Tracks not to scale

IT'S A BLAST!

ANSWERS TO BURNING QUESTIONS ABOUT EARTH'S VOLCANOES

THE 20TH CENTURY'S WORST

On June 6, 1912, Novarupta in Alaska erupted, sending smoke and ash 20 miles into the atmosphere. In Kodiak, a fishing village 100 miles away, ash piled up more than a foot deep, collapsing roofs and polluting air and water (thousands of birds and fish died, and water became undrinkable). By June 9, ash was falling on Seattle, Washington. By June 10, the ash had passed over Virginia. On June 17, it reached North Africa.

ONE OF THE MOST FAMOUS

On May 18, 1980, Mount St. Helens in Washington State erupted, issuing a 15-mile-high column of ash that lowered global temperatures by 0.1°F.

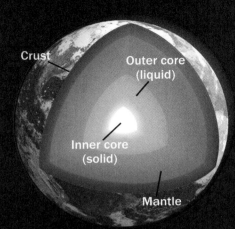

Crust
Outer core (liquid)
Inner core (solid)
Mantle

WHAT CAUSES VOLCANOES?

Earth's interior contains a core, mantle, and crust. The core, a solid iron center surrounded by liquid iron, is about 2,165 miles thick. Its temperature is believed to be at least 9,000°F.

The mantle consists of solid and semisolid rock up to 1,800 miles thick. Some of the rock melts; this is magma, and it collects in magma chambers. The upper mantle, being cooler and under less pressure, is brittle and cracked.

The crust is about 4 to 50 miles thick, thinnest beneath the oceans. With the upper mantle, it forms huge slabs called tectonic plates. Heat from the core causes these plates to move. They can collide, move apart, stretch, or rub. When enough pressure builds up, magma may find its way to the surface and come out in flows or sprays that also can contain gases, steam, ash, dust, cinders, and/ or rock. This is an eruption. Volcanic fragments and hot gases can race down the mountain at more than 300 miles per hour.

Lava is magma that has escaped from Earth's interior. Its temperature can be 570°F to 2,000°F or more when liquid. It becomes rock when it cools.

After many eruptions, as layers of lava, rock, and ash pile up and cool around a vent, a mountain or island forms.

The word "volcano" comes from **VULCAN,** the mythical Roman god of fire.

WHAT ARE "HOT SPOTS"?

A volcano can develop over a "hot spot" on a tectonic plate, possibly caused by a narrow column of very hot rock (mantle plume) that rises from deep within the mantle (A). As a plate moves, the volcano vent moves with it, leaving the mantle plume behind, belowground. Scientists think that the plume's hot magma then emerges at new spots along the moving plate, eventually forming a trail of volcanoes (B). This is how the Hawaiian and Galápagos islands were formed.

About 16.5 million years ago, a hot spot formed on the border of Nevada and Oregon. Today, it is at Yellowstone National Park in Wyoming, all because of plate movement.

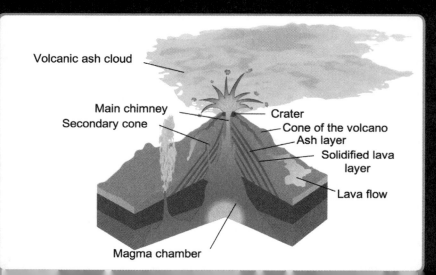

Volcanic ash cloud

Main chimney
Secondary cone

Crater
Cone of the volcano
Ash layer
Solidified lava layer

Lava flow

Magma chamber

HOW BAD CAN VOLCANOES BE?

Relatively mild eruptions occur if magma is hot, thin, and fluid, without much gas. Tall sprays of bright orange lava that last for minutes to hours can occur.

Violent eruptions occur if magma is somewhat cooler, thick, sticky, and gaseous. Magma and rock might be hurled into the air, break apart, and travel up to 3 miles. Shock waves from violent explosions can flatten forests around the vent. Toxic gases can contaminate plants and water and/or burn or suffocate life. Earthquakes can occur, as well as ocean tsunamis.

■ **TEPHRA** is volcanic material ejected into the air, from tiny ash particles to rocks as large as a house.

■ **LAHARS** are mudflows of tephra and water.

■ **LIGHTNING** can occur in eruptions when some parts of the ash cloud become negatively charged, while others become positively charged.

WHAT IS VOLCANIC ASH?

sh is tiny pieces of glass, minerals, crystals, and other rock fragments. Hard, abrasive, and slightly corrosive, it doesn't dissolve in water but will conduct electricity when wet.

Ash can make breathing difficult and phone lines go dead, stop planes and cars, cause power outages, collapse roofs, and kill vegetation. When blown over thousands of miles or into the stratosphere, it can lead to acid rain and cooler temperatures.

VOLCANOES on the ocean floor produce about 75 percent of the world's lava each year and are home to eyeless shrimp, tubeworms, **GIANT CLAMS**, and other unique life forms.

HOW LONG DO VOLCANOES LAST?

n **ACTIVE** volcano is one that is erupting or showing signs of unrest or has done so in recorded history and might erupt again.

A **DORMANT** volcano is one that is not active, but might erupt again.

An **EXTINCT** volcano erupted tens of thousands of years ago and is unlikely to do so again.

Earth has more than 1,500 potentially **ACTIVE** volcanoes on land. About 500 have **ERUPTED** in recorded history.

IS THERE ANYTHING GOOD ABOUT VOLCANOES?

ava, ash, and related materials eventually become fertile soil. Magma heats water underground, producing steam, which provides electricity and heat.

Volcanic rocks are sources of aluminum, copper, diamonds, gold, lead, silver, zinc, and other valuable minerals.

Ash in the atmosphere can cause brilliant sunrises and sunsets.

Earth's largest active volcano is **MAUNA LOA** in Hawaii. It rises about 56,000 feet above the ocean floor (13,680 feet above sea level) and erupts relatively mildly every 2 to 3 years.

In Hawaiian legend, green **PERIDOT CRYSTALS** found in volcanic ash were the tears of the volcano goddess, Pele.

WHAT DO YOU CALL A VOLCANO EXPERT?

volcanologist is a person who measures, maps, and studies volcanoes and collects samples of rock and lava—all to learn how volcanoes form and if or when they will erupt.

MAKE A VOLCANO

This is messy, so try it outdoors and wear old clothes!

YOU WILL NEED:

tarp, newspapers, or vinyl tablecloth
old cake pan or tin pie plate
small empty plastic soda bottle
modeling clay or play dough
3 tablespoons baking soda
½ cup water

a few drops liquid dishwashing detergent
a few drops red and orange food coloring
½ cup vinegar
funnel

1. Cover an old table or the ground with the tarp.

2. Place the pan in the center of your work area. Place the bottle in the middle of the pan.

3. Pile modeling clay up around the sides of the bottle, shaping it to look like a volcano; leave the top of the bottle free of clay.

4. Insert the funnel into the bottleneck and pour the baking soda into the bottle. Add the water, detergent, and food coloring.

5. Pour the vinegar into the bottle through the funnel, then remove the funnel and step back! Your volcano should erupt with red-orange bubbles.

WHY THIS WORKS

Vinegar mixing with the baking soda produces bubbles of carbon dioxide (CO_2). As the CO_2 expands, it increases the pressure in the bottle, forcing the liquid and gas to come out the top, or vent.

This American tradition has an international pedigree.*

Hot-diggity, *Dog-ziggity,*

Yum or Yech?

Visitors to the 2012 Canadian National Exhibition were the first to see and sample Ontario-based Maple Lodge Farms' hot dog inside a chocolate-covered éclair, topped with whipped cream and sprinkles.

The origin of the term "hot dog" is shrouded in a cloud of steam. Here are a few theories:

■ Modern history gives Germans credit for inventing the sausage. Some say that it was folks in Frankfurt-am-Main in the 1400s; others say that it was a butcher in Coburg in the 1600s. Residents of Vienna, Austria, whose city is spelled "Wien" in German, claim to have first called the hot dog a "wiener."

■ In 1901, a food vendor selling steamed sausages wrapped in bread rolls at the New York Polo Grounds invited customers to try his "dachshund sausages." When cartoonist Tad Dorgan saw and heard the vendor, he sketched an illustration of a puppy in a bun and, due to his inability to spell "dachshund," dubbed it a "hot dog."

F O O D

HOT DOGS!

*PEDIGREE?
This word refers to a family history or origin and is commonly used to describe a dog's background.

Did You Know?

A **dogleg** is a sharp angle or turn.

The **dog watch** aboard ship is a 2-hour watch that occurs twice a day, from 4:00 to 6:00 and 6:00 to 8:00 P.M.

A **dog-eared** book is one whose page corners are turned down.

■ Adolf Gehring, a food vendor at a baseball game in St. Louis, Missouri, once served so many fans that he ran out of food, except for bread. He bought sausages from a butcher, wrapped the links in the bread, and called each one a "meat sandwich," until a customer requested "one of those hot dogs."

PLATE UP A DOG TEAM

Turn hot dogs into an animal menagerie in minutes. (Ask an adult to help.)

- -

YOU WILL NEED:

hot dogs
a knife
toothpicks
mustard, ketchup, and relish

cooked spinach pasta
raisins
uncooked spaghetti

- -

■ Put hot dogs into a boiling pot of water, cover, and remove from heat. Let stand for 7 minutes, then remove hot dogs to a plate.

Bunny Dog

■ Cut a boiled hot dog in half crosswise.

■ Starting at the cut end, slice each tube halfway down lengthwise (one becomes the head with ears and one becomes the feet).

■ If necessary, use toothpicks to keep the legs and ears spread apart. Toothpick the head on top of legs as shown.

■ Use raisins on toothpicks for eyes and mustard for nose.

Octopus Dog

- Slice a boiled hot dog all the way through for about two-thirds of its length.
- Roll the hot dog slightly and make another similar slice, then roll again and make a third slice. You should now have six "tentacles" and a head.
- Set your octopus on a bed of spinach pasta "seaweed" and use mustard or ketchup to make a face.

Jellyfish Dogs

- Cut an uncooked hot dog into 1-inch pieces.
- Stick six strands of uncooked spaghetti into one end of each piece.
- Place in boiling water and cook for 7 to 8 minutes, then carefully remove onto a bed of relish "seaweed."

2009 contest winners celebrate!

Champion Dog Food-ies

The most popular hot dog–eating championship might be Nathan's Famous Fourth of July International Hot Dog Eating Contest, held on Coney Island in Brooklyn, New York. Conducted every year since 1916 (with the exceptions of 1941 and 1971), the event runs for only 10 minutes, attracts more than 40,000 fans, involves 30 eaters, and awards more than $20,000 in cash prizes.

The men's and women's winners in 2014 were seven-time champ Joey "Jaws" Chestnut from San Jose, California, who consumed 61 hot dogs and buns, and Miki Sudo from Las Vegas, Nevada, who put away 34 dogs and buns.

No one knows for sure how Native Americans discovered maple syrup. One legend tells of a chief who stuck his tomahawk into a maple tree one spring night. In the morning, he pulled it out and went off hunting. His wife had placed a container under the tree, and the clear, watery sap dripped into it.

Later, she needed water to cook the meat for dinner. Thinking that the sap in the container was water, she used it. As it cooked, the water evaporated until syrup was left. The sweet meat was the best they had ever tasted, and they ate every drop of the gooey treat. They told their friends, and then everyone began cooking their meat in maple sap. Soon they began making sap into maple sugar so that they could enjoy maple sweetness all year long.

A Sweet DISCOVERY

A Squirrel Tap

A squirrel will chew the bottom of a maple branch in the spring. When sap starts dripping, the squirrel sometimes hangs upside down by its feet to drink it.

FROM TREE TO TABLE

The northeastern United States and southeastern Canada are the only places in the world where sugar maples grow naturally and weather conditions are right to harvest maple sap.

In the early spring, folks who make maple syrup drill a small hole about 1 inch deep in the tree trunk and push a small spout into it. This is called tapping the tree. A maple tree should be 40 years old or 12 inches across the trunk before it is tapped. The sap goes out through the spout and into a pail that hangs on the tree, or it travels through plastic tubing to a barrel or tank.

SUGAR MAPLE

THE SPEED OF SAP

On a warm day, a tree may drip two drops of sap per second. If the weather is cool, the drip will be slower. When it's very cold or very warm, day or night, the sap won't run at all.

Did You Know?

■ Native Americans taught the early settlers how to make maple sugar. In colonial times, some people survived on maple sugar when other food was scarce.

■ Maple sugar was the most common sweetener in the northern United States and Canada until the late 1800s, when white sugar took its place.

■ Some people tap birch trees in the spring to make birch syrup, but the favorite flavor is maple.

Beginning usually in February, when the weather is just right—the nighttime temperature is in the 20° to 30°F range and the days are sunny and calm, with the temperature above 40°F—sap flows most easily from the tree. Lasting for 4 to 6 weeks, the flow is called a "sap run," although it actually just drips off and on.

Folks bring the clear sap to a maple sugaring house, where it is boiled, or cooked down, for hours in large flat pans, until it becomes a thick, golden syrup. (Nothing is added to the sap.) More than 40 gallons of sap are needed to make 1 gallon of maple syrup.

As the weather grows warmer, each batch of syrup turns out a little darker in color and stronger in flavor than the last. The difference in each batch determines its grade. Boiling maple sap past the syrup stage causes it to turn into sugar. This can be shaped into candies. One of the most popular shapes is a maple tree leaf.

MAKE IT MAPLE

One of the most common ways to have maple syrup is to pour it on pancakes or waffles. Here are some other sweet ways to enjoy it!

MAPLE MILK SHAKE

1/2 cup maple syrup
a few drops of vanilla extract
a half-full gallon jug of milk with top

■ Add the maple syrup and vanilla to the milk. Put the top on the milk jug tightly and shake well. **Makes 8 glasses** (8 ounces each).

MAPLE SAUCE

1 cup maple syrup
1/2 cup marshmallow cream

■ Combine the syrup and cream in a bowl and beat with a hand beater or whisk until it is thoroughly mixed. Serve it on ice cream, cake, or pudding. **Makes about 1½ cups.**

MAPLE BUTTER

Try this on toast or warm muffins.

1/2 cup butter, softened
2 tablespoons maple syrup

■ Put the butter and maple syrup into a bowl and mix until the syrup combines with the butter. Store in a covered container in the refrigerator. **Makes about ½ cup.**

MAPLE GRANOLA

Ask an adult for help, if necessary.

1/4 cup vegetable oil
2/3 cup maple syrup
1/4 cup sesame seeds
1/2 cup shredded unsweetened coconut
3 1/2 cups rolled oats (not instant)
1/2 cup chopped almonds (optional)
1 cup raisins, dried cranberries, and/or dried cherries

■ Preheat the oven to 225°F. Line a rimmed baking sheet with parchment paper.
■ In a bowl, stir to combine the oil, maple syrup, sesame seeds, coconut, oats, and almonds, if using. Spread on the prepared baking sheet.
■ Put the baking sheet into the oven. Bake until the granola is golden brown, up to about 1½ hours. Remove it from the oven every 15 minutes and stir the mixture so that it cooks evenly.
■ When it's done, transfer the warm, toasted granola to a bowl. Be careful. It will be hot!
■ Stir in the dried fruit, then set aside to cool. Store in a tightly sealed container at room temperature. **Makes about 8 cups.**

NUTS

Are You Allergic?

Many kids are allergic to peanuts and other nuts. Nuts can cause difficulty breathing, stomachache, vomiting, itchy rashes, and/or swelling. There is no special medicine for nut or peanut allergies, and most people do not outgrow them.

If you are allergic to nuts:

• Avoid foods that include nuts. Read food labels. Nuts are added to many foods as fillers or thickeners.

• Tell your friends, family, teachers, and coaches, and, when you eat in a restaurant, your server.

TO YOU!

Are you hungry when you get home from school? Need a snack for your lunch box? Try nuts!

FOR HEALTH NUTS

Nuts contain a big dose of healthy fats and nutrients, and they can boost your energy and brainpower.

- Low-calorie nuts include almonds, cashews, and pistachios.

- High-calorie nuts include macadamia nuts and pecans.

TREAT YOURSELF

Combine nuts with dried cranberries or raisins for a tasty snack.

Sprinkle chopped nuts on your breakfast cereal and yogurt.

Mix nuts into your favorite muffin recipe.

Almonds

Almonds are native to the Middle East but are now grown in California and other regions with a Mediterranean climate. Almonds grow on small, bushy trees and are related to plums and peaches. The almond is the seed of an inedible, plum-size fruit; the nut is inside a hard shell (the pit).

● **Children in Japan snack on slivered almonds and dried sardines.**

Q: What did the nut say when it sneezed?

A: Cashew!

CASHEWS

Cashews are native to Brazil, but are now grown in Vietnam, India, and many African countries. Cashews are related to poison ivy! The cashew nut is a seed that grows on the outside of a fruit called a cashew apple. The cashew's double shell contains a toxic oil, urushiol, which is also found in poison ivy—so cashew oil can blister your skin like poison ivy oil does. The shells and oils are removed in processing, and then the nuts are roasted or steamed to remove any traces of the oil.

● **Cashew oil is used in varnishes and paints.**

● **One study claims that the oil can be used to kill mosquito larvae.**

● **Cashew apples can be used for juices and jams. They are also used in Indian cooking to sweeten curries.**

MACADAMIA NUTS

Macadamia nuts are native to Australia and grow in tropical areas. In 1881, macadamia trees were imported to Hawaii and used for reforestation. Today, Hawaii grows about 90 percent of the world's supply.

- The macadamia tree is named for John Macadam, a professor at the University of Melbourne (Australia).

- Macadamia trees grow to be 30 to 40 feet tall and almost as wide, and the nut has the hardest shell of any nut.

- Macadamia nuts are toxic to dogs.

Q: How do you make a pecan laugh?

A: Crack it up!

Pecans

Pecan trees are native to North America. Before European settlers arrived, Native Americans ate and traded pecans. The name "pecan" comes from the Algonquian word *paccan*, which means "a nut with a shell so hard that it must be cracked with a stone." Pecan trees are huge, usually ranging in height from 70 to 100 feet, and some reach 150 feet or more! Of the more than 1,000 varieties of pecans, many are named for Native American tribes, such as Cheyenne, Mohawk, and Sioux.

- George Washington and Thomas Jefferson planted pecan trees in the 1700s. Washington called them Mississippi nuts. Jefferson imported trees from Louisiana for Monticello, his Virginia estate.

- In 2002, NASA astronaut Peggy Whitson received a pecan pie from her husband while in space!

PEANUTS

Peanuts are native to central South America. Today, China, India, the United States, and parts of Africa grow the most peanuts. Peanuts are legumes and related to peas; they are sometimes called "groundnuts" because they are actually formed under the ground.

● **George Washington Carver began researching peanuts in 1903 and introduced them as crops to farmers in the South. He discovered over 300 uses for peanuts, such as in shaving cream, leather dye, ink, and shoe polish.**

● **Ancient Incas in South America first ground peanuts to make peanut butter, which was introduced to the United States at the 1904 Universal Exposition (World's Fair) in St. Louis, Missouri.**

● **Arachibutyrophobia (a-RACK-i-byew-ti-ra-FO-bee-a) is the fear of getting peanut butter stuck to the roof of your mouth.**

Q: What do you call a peanut in a spacesuit?

A: An astro-nut.

Pine Nuts

About 18 species of pine trees grown in Asia, Europe, and North America produce cones with seeds, which are the nuts, large enough to be harvested for food. Also known as pignolia (peen-YOH-lee-a), pine nuts have many uses:

● **In Europe, pine nuts are added to savory foods, pastries, and biscuits. Italian-invented pesto, which is often served on pasta, includes pine nuts.**

● **Pine nuts are eaten by songbirds, squirrels, chipmunks, and bears, as well as people.**

Pistachios

Pistachios are native to the Middle East. Today, they are grown in California and regions with a desert climate. Pistachios are related to the mango, and the nuts are the seeds of a plumlike fruit. Humans have been eating pistachios for at least 9,000 years. Early explorers and traders carried pistachios because they are nutritious and can be stored for long periods.

- In China, pistachios are called "the happy nut." In Iran, pistachios are known as the "smiling nut." Pistachios are also known as the "green almond."

- Years ago, pistachios were dyed red to cover stains on the shells. Today, it is not as common to dye pistachios.

WALNUTS

English walnuts originated in ancient Persia, where they were reserved for royalty. Franciscan monks in California first grew walnuts in the late 1700s. China and California produce 75 percent of the world's supply.

Black walnuts are native to North America and grow mainly in the eastern and central United States. They belong to the hickory family. Black walnuts are expensive, and black walnut wood is valued for its beauty and quality.

- Ancient Greeks called walnuts *karyon*, meaning "head," likely because the shell resembles a human skull and the nut inside looks like a brain!

- English walnuts have a soft, thin shell. Black walnuts have a powdery black shell that stains hands.

Let's Do Lunch

Did you know that prior to the 19th century, lunch was a small meal eaten at any time of the day or night? Make these fun and tasty lunch items for school or a picnic or just enjoy them at your kitchen counter at any time of the day you please.

CHOCOLATE BANANA SMOOTHIE

1 cup milk or milk substitute (such as almond milk)
1 tablespoon honey
1 tablespoon cocoa powder
1 frozen banana, cut into chunks

YOU WILL ALSO NEED:
blender
1 large container with lid

1. Put all of the ingredients into a blender. Blend until smooth.

2. Put the smoothie into a container with a lid if bringing to school.

Makes 1 serving.

HAM-AND-CHEESE KABOBS

1 string cheese, cut into rounds
1 thick slice of ham, cut into cubes
6 to 8 cherry tomatoes

YOU WILL ALSO NEED:
2 wooden skewers

1. Alternately slide cheese, ham, and tomatoes onto each skewer, then enjoy!

Makes 1 serving.

RICE AND VEGGIE BALLS

⅓ **cup finely chopped broccoli**
⅓ **cup fresh or frozen peas, thawed**
⅓ **cup shredded carrots**
1 teaspoon canola oil
1 tablespoon sesame seeds
1 teaspoon sesame oil
pinch of sea salt
1 cup warm cooked rice

YOU WILL ALSO NEED:
skillet
2 plastic sandwich bags

1. Stir-fry the veggies in canola oil in a skillet over medium-high heat.

2. Remove the skillet from the heat; add the sesame seeds, sesame oil, and salt to the veggies; and stir.

3. Put the vegetables into a large bowl, add the warm rice, and stir.

4. Put each of your hands into a sandwich bag and form little balls out of the rice mixture.

5. If you don't want to eat them right away, refrigerate for later.

Makes 2 servings.

PEANUT BUTTER AND JELLY SUSHI

2 slices bread
2 tablespoons peanut or
  sunflower butter
2 tablespoons jelly or jam

YOU WILL ALSO NEED:
knife
rolling pin or canned good

1. Cut the crusts off the bread and flatten each slice with a rolling pin.

2. Put peanut butter on half of each slice and jelly on the other, then roll the slices into logs.

3. Cut each log into four or five pieces of "sushi."

Makes 1 serving.

HUMMUS PIZZA

Use your favorite vegetable or meat toppings with or instead of any of these ingredients.

1 pita bread or wrap
3 to 4 tablespoons hummus
½ cup shredded mozzarella cheese
¼ cup chopped bell pepper
1 small tomato, sliced
6 slices regular or turkey pepperoni

1. If you wish, heat the pita bread in a 350°F oven for 5 minutes.

2. Make a "pizza" by spreading the hummus on the pita and then adding the toppings.

Makes 1 serving.

FROZEN FRUIT CUPS

1 cup frozen cherries
1 cup frozen blueberries
6 ounces frozen orange juice concentrate, thawed
1 can (20 ounces) crushed pineapple, with juice
¼ cup water

YOU WILL ALSO NEED:
8 containers (1 cup each) with lids

1. Put all of the ingredients into a large bowl and stir.

2. Divide the mixture among the containers. Fill almost to the top; the fruit will expand when it freezes.

3. Put the lids on the cups and place them in the freezer until the fruit is frozen.

4. Thaw slightly before eating.

Makes 8 servings.

APPLE CHIPS

3 apples (try Granny Smith, Winesap, or Honey Crisp)
2 teaspoons sugar
1 teaspoon cinnamon

YOU WILL ALSO NEED:
2 baking sheets
parchment paper or 2 silicone baking mats
spatula
1 large container with lid

1. Preheat the oven to 200°F. Line two baking sheets with parchment paper.

2. Cut the apples into very thin slices.

3. In a small bowl, mix together the sugar and cinnamon.

4. Place the apple slices on the lined baking sheets in a single layer and sprinkle them with about half of the sugar–cinnamon mixture.

5. Bake for 1 hour, then remove from the oven and flip the slices over with a spatula.

6. Sprinkle the slices with the remaining sugar–cinnamon mixture.

7. Bake for 1½ hours more, then turn off the oven and leave the apples inside for 1 hour.

8. Store the apple chips in a container with a tight lid.

Makes 3 servings.

THE BRAIN

Your Own Personal Supercomputer

What works **24/7**, is faster than the **fastest computer,** and weighs about 3 pounds?

YOUR BRAIN!

Each part of the brain has a **special job** to do:

The biggest part of the brain, the portion that you use when you're thinking about how to solve a puzzle, do a math problem, or play a game, is the **cerebrum** (ser-REE-brum). It stores your short- and long-term memories and helps you to make decisions that require reasoning and making choices, like what gift to choose for a friend's birthday.

The cerebrum has two halves. The right half helps you to think about music and colors. The left half helps you with math, reasoning, and speech. The right half controls the left side of your body, and the left half controls your right side.

The small part of the brain that connects the brain to your spinal cord is the **brain stem.** It controls the muscles in your heart, lungs, and stomach that you need to keep blood pumping throughout your body, to breathe, and to digest food.

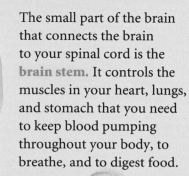

You depend on your **cerebellum** (ser-eh-BEH-lum) any time you move. The cerebellum is much smaller than the cerebrum, yet it controls balance and muscle coordination and helps you to stand upright. When you're skating, swimming, or riding a skateboard, your cerebellum is working hard, telling your muscles what to do.

The **pituitary gland** is about the size of a pea and produces hormones that help you to grow. So, if the jacket that you wore last winter is too small for you, it's likely because the pituitary gland is doing its job.

The **hypothalamus** (high-po-THAL-ah-muss) maintains your body temperature and helps to keep you cool in summer and warm in winter. If you become too hot, your hypothalamus tells your body to sweat to cool you down. If you're cold, your hypothalamus will start you shivering. Sweating and shivering are your body's attempt to keep you at a normal temperature of about 98.6°F.

The **amygdala** (a-MIG-da-la) is about the size of an almond, yet it is responsible for your emotions like anger and fear. When you look at a person's face, the amygdala helps you to get clues about how that person is feeling.

You have about 100 billion **neurons** (NYOU-rons) in your brain and many more throughout your body. These microscopic nerve cells send and receive chemical and electrical signals nonstop, even when you're asleep. The signals travel along tiny neuron highways.

Suppose you touch a hot stove. The neurons in your fingers and hand send the information up the neuron network to your brain. The neurons in your brain receive the message and send information back to the motor neurons in your arm and hands, and you pull back your hand. This happens in a flash because motor neurons relay this information as quickly as 268 miles per hour.

is **75%** water.

uses about **20%** of the total oxygen and blood in your body.

grows about three times its size in the first year of life and stops growing at about **age 18.**

processes about **70,000** thoughts every day and creates new connections between **neurons** every time you learn something new.

About That Gray Matter

YOUR BRAIN . . .

contains **five times** as much information as an encyclopedia. Some scientists believe that the brain can store up to **1,000** terabytes (about 1,000 **trillion** bytes) of information.

is called "gray matter" because the **cortex,** the outer layer of the **cerebrum,** is gray.

contains **100,000** miles of blood vessels.

doesn't **feel pain** because it doesn't contain pain receptors. When you have a headache, most likely the **nerve endings** in your neck or face are feeling the pain. Nerve endings throughout your body feel pain and send that **message** to your **brain.**

Get Smart!

To keep your brain in shape, give it a good workout. Each time you have a new idea or learn something new, the neurons in your brain create new connections that help to make you smarter. Here are some fun activities to keep making those connections:

- **Put together a jigsaw puzzle**
- **Read**
- **Draw or paint**
- **Play an instrument**
- **Learn a new game or sport**

TAKE CARE OF YOUR BRAIN!

EAT A BALANCED DIET that includes fresh fruit, vegetables, and whole grains. Limit the amount of sugar that you eat. Although you may get an extra boost of energy right after eating sugary foods, it is usually followed by a feeling of lack of energy.

EXERCISE REGULARLY. It makes your heart pump more oxygen throughout your body.

DON'T SKIP BREAKFAST. Studies show that students who haven't eaten for several hours do not do as well on tests as students who have had breakfast. Be sure to include protein in your breakfast. Scientists say that a breakfast of baked beans on toast has been shown to help keep you smart.

DRINK PLENTY OF WATER. If you don't drink enough water, you can become dehydrated, which can upset the balance of chemicals and hormones in your brain.

GET PLENTY OF SLEEP. A good night's sleep "repairs" the brain and keeps you alert the next day.

ALWAYS WEAR A HELMET when biking, skateboarding, or skiing.

B·R·A·I·N·T·E·A·S·E·R·S

1. A famous magician claimed to be able to throw a ping-pong ball so that it would go a short distance, come to a complete stop, and then reverse itself. He also added that he would not bounce the ball off any object or tie anything to it. How could he perform this trick?

2. Mary's parents have four children; three are named Nana, Nene, and Nini. What is the fourth child's name?

3. What are the next three letters in the following sequence?

J, F, M, A, M, J, J, A, __, __, __

3. S, O, N. The sequence is the first letter of the months of the year. September, October, and November are the next in the sequence.

2. Mary

1. He threw the ball straight up in the air.

Did You Know?

Because your brain can tell the difference between an unexpected touch and your own touch, it's impossible to tickle yourself.

I like nonsense; it wakes up the brain cells.

–Theodor Geisel ("Dr. Seuss"; 1904–91)

BRAIN JOKES

Q. Why didn't the brain want to take a bath?

A. It didn't want to get brainwashed.

Q. What do you call a hat for a brain?

A. A thinking cap.

Q. What did the doctor say to the man who had an elephant sitting on his head?

A. It looks like you have a lot on your mind.

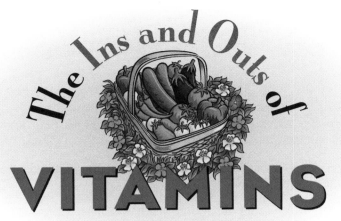

The Ins and Outs of

VITAMINS

Getting enough vitamins and minerals isn't hard. All that you really need to do is eat a healthy diet. Build it around fruit and vegetables (8 to 10 servings a day), whole-grain breads and cereals, beans, low-fat poultry and meat, nonfried fish, milk, cheese, and yogurt.

Here's what vitamins do and where they are found in your food:

VITAMIN	WHAT IT DOES	WHERE IT IS
Vitamin A	• good for your eyesight • helps you see in the dark • helps fight infections • helps bone growth	milk, cheese, eggs, liver, fish oil, yellow fruit, dark-green and yellow veggies
B Vitamins	• help make red blood cells • help make energy and release it	whole grains (wheat and oats), fish and seafood, meat, poultry, eggs, dairy products, leafy green veggies, beans and peas, citrus fruit
Vitamin C	• keeps gums and muscles healthy • helps heal cuts • helps body resist infection	citrus fruit and juices, berries, tomatoes, peppers, broccoli, potatoes, cauliflower, cantaloupe
Vitamin D	• makes strong bones and teeth	milk, egg yolks, fish
Vitamin E	• helps make red blood cells • keeps tissues in eyes, skin, and liver healthy • protects lungs from pollution	whole grains (wheat and oats), wheat germ, leafy green veggies, sardines, nuts, egg yolks
Vitamin K	• helps blood to clot	leafy green veggies, pork, liver, dairy products

GET UP AND GO!

Now that you have all of that energy from eating your healthy diet, you are probably looking for ways to burn it off, right? You might be surprised to know that just doing some chores around the house can burn off quite a bit of energy.

Look at the chart below. The column on the left lists the activity, the middle column tells you how many calories you will burn per minute for every pound of your body weight, and the column on the right lists an activity that would burn the same amount. So, if you weigh 100 pounds and are shoveling snow, you are burning 3.8 calories each minute, the same amount you would use in playing golf.

Chopping wood	0.060	Playing football
Mowing lawn	0.051	Horseback riding (trot)
Shoveling snow	0.038	Golfing
Painting walls	0.035	Walking (normal pace)
Weeding garden	0.033	Playing Ping-Pong
Shopping for food	0.028	Cycling at 5.5 mph
Mopping floors	0.028	Fishing
Raking lawn	0.025	Bowling

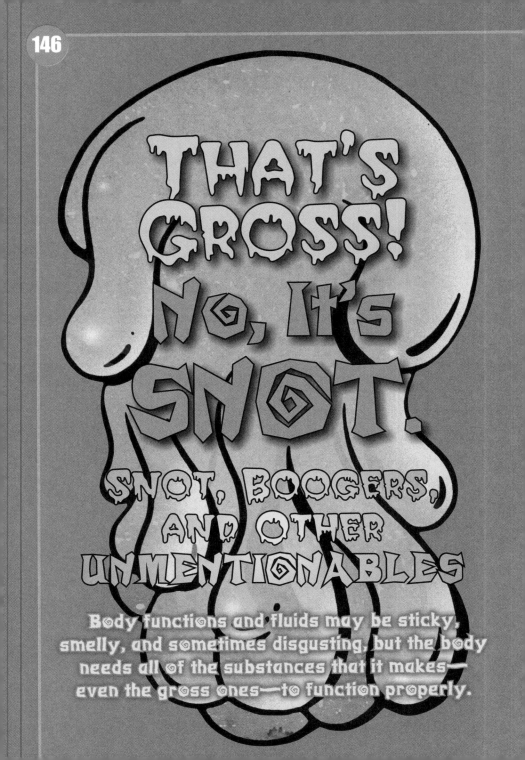

THAT'S GROSS! NO, It's SNOT.

SNOT, BOOGERS, AND OTHER UNMENTIONABLES

Body functions and fluids may be sticky, smelly, and sometimes disgusting, but the body needs all of the substances that it makes— even the gross ones—to function properly.

MUCUS or SNOT ?

Everyone has experienced a drippy nose. What exactly is that gooey stuff that runs out? It's mucus. Mucus membranes line the inside of your nose and sinuses. The mucus itself is 95 percent water, 2 to 3 percent salt, and 2 percent mucin (a special kind of protein). It also contains antibodies and enzymes that help to kill bacteria and viruses.

Mucus membranes secrete snot to protect your body from things such as dirt, pollen, dust, and germs. The mucus acts as a trap to catch junk that you inhale so that it doesn't get into your lungs and make you sick. When mucus dries up, it turns into a booger. The best way to get rid of one of these is to blow your nose. Remember: Boogers are germ traps and you don't want them on your fingers.

If germs do sneak by, you'll probably get a runny nose because your body's reaction is to go into mucus-making overdrive. The extra mucus helps to wash away the germs. Mucus is usually clear in color. If it changes to a color, such as white, yellow, or green, you might have an infection.

HONORABLE MENTIONABLES

- Your nose and sinuses make about a quart of mucus every day.
- When you sneeze, the air and snot in your nose come out at up to 100 miles per hour!
- Kings and queens were using the term "snot" as far back as the 1600s.

BURPS

Have you ever been at the dining room table and suddenly burped? This may not be polite, but it is natural. (It is polite to say "Excuse me.") Burping is an involuntary reflex action.

Your stomach is full of digestive juices to break down whatever you eat. If a lot of air travels to your stomach with the food (this often happens when you eat too fast or have carbonated drinks), pressure will build in your stomach and it will expand. Burping releases most of the air and other gases from your stomach. The noise that you make when you burp is actually your epiglottis (the flap that hangs in the back of your throat) vibrating!

15

Honorable Mentionables

On average, people burp about 15 times a day.

"Eructation" is another word for burping.

In some cultures, burping after a meal is considered polite. It is a compliment toward the cook's culinary skills.

Stinky Gas

Not all of the air in your stomach escapes by burping. Some of it travels to your intestines and gets released out through your bottom. (When this happens to you—and it happens to everybody—say "Excuse me.")

Air that you ingest while eating contains gases such as nitrogen and oxygen. These gases travel through your digestive system with your food. When the food gets to your large intestine, more smelly gases form from the breakdown of undigested food. The gases need to escape, and the quickest route is through your anus.

Certain foods—beans, broccoli, cauliflower, onions, white bread, and fried foods, for example—can cause excess gas in your body. If you eat something that makes you feel uncomfortably gassy but the gas won't come out, take a walk. Exercise helps gas and food to move through your digestive system.

Honorable Mentionables

If you passed gas in outer space, you would release enough pressure to push you forward.

On average, people pass gas about 14 times a day.

Herring (fish) pass gas to communicate and keep their group (or "school") together in dark waters.

A WHALE OF

True or not, it's quite a yarn!

IN FEBRUARY 1891, James Bartley was off the coast of the Falkland Islands (near the east coast of South America) aboard the whaling ship *Star of the East*. One day, James found himself in the water, having been aboard a small boat that had been overturned by a large bull whale wounded by a harpoon thrust.

When a rescue boat arrived, James and another crewman were missing.

Later that afternoon, two other boats saw the same bull whale, captured it, and drew it alongside. According to the ship's captain, Mike Dolan, this happened:

WITH LINES AROUND the whale's body, the crew hoisted it onto the ship. They were carving up the carcass when a few men noticed something moving inside the whale's stomach. Working feverishly, with sharp knives, they slit it open and found James, quivering and unconscious, his skin snow-white.

Spashing salt water over the still form of James, they seemed to revive him. After he had been washed off and had a few sips of a beverage forced through his pale lips, he was carried to the ship's cabin.

After 2 weeks of hovering near death, he finally recovered—and told a weird tale.

A TALE

REMEMBERING BEING thrown high in the air when the giant whale struck the boat with its tail, James said that he had heard a rumbling sound like a train roaring over a bridge. He imagined that the noise was caused by the whale pounding the sea. In the darkness, his hand touched a slick substance that yielded to his feeble efforts to escape. Then he was drawn forward into a chamber where there was more air.

Each time he tried to crawl forward in the black chamber, some invisible force seemed to draw him back. Then his terrible plight dawned on him: He was inside the body of a whale! Weak from strain and the heat, he collapsed and remembered nothing until he awakened on Captain Mike's ship.

James's skin never regained its natural color, but he regained his strength and lived for many years, continuing to fish where he had almost met his doom.

No proof of this tale has ever surfaced. Do you think it sounds fishy? Share your thoughts at Almanac4kids.com/TellUs/WhaleTale.

WILD ADVENTURERS

The Longest, Hardest-Ever Walk to Work

Luckily, he had to take it only once.

O N SEPTEMBER 12, 1884, 25-year-old Charles F. Lummis got out of his bed in Cincinnati, Ohio; put on a white flannel shirt, knickerbockers (pants that are cuffed just below the knee), red knee-high stockings, dress shoes, a canvas coat, and a wide-brimmed hat; and walked out of his house. He did not stop walking, except to eat, sleep, and occasionally get a few days' rest, until he reached Los Angeles, California, a distance of more than 2,200 miles.

Charles had gathered supplies in the preceding days. A Bowie knife hung from his belt, in which he had tucked $300 in gold coins. He had stuffed the 23 pockets of his coat with canned food, fishing tackle, and writing supplies, among other things. He had shipped a bedroll to Kansas City, where he would pick it up; the coat was big enough to use as a blanket, if necessary.

He was walking for, and to, a job. He had told the publisher of the *Los Angeles Times,* Harrison G. Otis, that he would write about his adventures every week and send the story to the newspaper for publication, if Otis would give him a job when he arrived.

C HARLES WALKED from 30 to 50 miles each day, then wrote about it at night by campfire light. During the first week of the trip, his feet blistered into excruciating stumps. He "cured" these, as he did most ailments, by doing nothing.

His longest trek was the 82 miles from Ellsworth to Ellis, Kansas, which he walked in 21 hours. He would have done it in less time, he claimed, if he hadn't fallen asleep when he stopped to rest.

Several hundred miles from Los Angeles, Charles fell off a 20-foot cliff and was knocked unconscious. When he awoke, his left arm was broken

SEVERAL HUNDRED MILES FROM LOS ANGELES, CHARLES FELL OFF A 20-FOOT CLIFF AND WAS KNOCKED UNCONSCIOUS.

below the elbow. The muscles and tendons had turned blue and bone stuck out of his flesh. He knew he would lose his arm if he did not set it immediately. In desperation, he tied one end of his canteen strap to his swollen wrist and the other end to a tree. Then he clenched his teeth and threw himself back from the tree as hard as he could. He blacked out from the pain, but when he woke up, the arm was set. He made simple splints and staggered 52 miles to Winslow, Arizona.

T MIDNIGHT on February 1, 1885, 143 days after leaving Cincinnati, Charles, with his broken arm in a sling, crossed into Los Angeles. The next day, he started work as the newspaper's first city editor.

He Walked on Air

... while kindness kept him grounded.

TIGHTROPE WALKER Jay Cochrane did not believe in using safety nets. "Nets are for two things," he said—for catching fish and for keeping his grandmother's hair in place.

Born in Saint John, New Brunswick, on May 1, 1944, Jay became fascinated by tightrope walking at age 8, when his mother took him to the circus. After that, people often saw him walking on ledges around town. At 14, he ran away and joined a circus in Toronto. His first job was sweeping up after horses and elephants. In his free time, he learned how to wire walk from a performer named Struppi Hanneford. Soon, Jay was performing before big audiences. Jay walked a wire that was the width of a bicycle tire, while carrying a balancing pole 39 feet long.

Jay had one serious accident: When he was 21, he fell 90 feet onto a concrete floor, breaking his pelvis, legs, feet, and ribs—all because someone had not tightened a bolt properly. (In the future, before a walk he would check all of the bolts, wires, and fasteners himself.) During the 4 years that it took for him to recover, he earned a college degree in structural engineering, which proved useful in the design of his wires.

Jay's first walk after the accident was 500 feet above the ground between two Toronto skyscrapers. For a few moments he was terrified, but he completed the walk successfully and went on to perform many record-setting feats:

■ In Toronto at the Canadian National Exhibition in 1972, he walked almost 2½ miles on a wire 120 feet in the air by going back and forth (41 crossings!) on a 300-foot rope.

■ At an amusement park in Puerto Rico in 1981, Jay lived in the air for 21 days. Twice each day, he walked a tightrope. He spent the rest of the time on a small platform (with a portable toilet). He didn't sleep much, fearing that he might fall.

■ In China in 1995, he set up and walked the the longest high wire ever. It was 2,098 feet long, suspended 1,340 feet above the Yangtze River. He became a hero in China, and the authorities issued a postage stamp in his honor.

■ In Las Vegas, Nevada, in 1998, Jay walked an 800-foot-long, 300-foot-high wire while blindfolded.

■ Beginning on July 6, 2012, and for the next 80 days, he walked a 1,300-foot-long wire 750 feet above the ground between two hotels in Niagara Falls.

J AY USED HIS skill not only to entertain people, but also to raise money for children's charities and spread a message of kindness: "In the mirror each morning, when you look back at yourself, tell yourself to make a positive difference in people's lives." He died on October 30, 2013.

HOW FUN IS FUNAMBULISM?

A "funambulist" is a tightrope walker. The word comes from two Latin words: *funis*, meaning "rope," and *ambulare*, meaning "to walk."

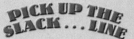

PICK UP THE SLACK . . . LINE

Slacklining is a hot sport among kids everywhere. It's done on a length of nylon-lined tubular webbing about 1 inch in diameter loosely strung between two fixed points a few inches off the ground. Walkers use their arms (not a pole) to maintain balance. It takes practice and concentration: Being nylon, a slackline is springy and sways in every direction, but with friends to lean on while learning, kids who get the hang of it love it!

The Yankee Leaper

He took jumping to new heights.

A S A BOY in Pawtucket, Rhode Island, in the early 1800s, Sam Patch loved to jump. At age 7, he took a job at a cotton mill. In his free time, he jumped off the mill's roof into the waters near the falls that powered the mill. One day, he made a 100-foot jump, feet first, from the six-story mill into "the pot," or bottom, of Pawtucket Falls. Soon people were calling him "The Yankee Leaper."

In 1827, Sam moved to New Jersey to be a boss at a mill. He continued to jump. In September, he plunged from the Clinton Bridge into the Great Falls of the Passaic River in Paterson, a drop of about 75 feet, as many spectators watched. The following July 4, he did it again. Ten months later, he leaped from the mast of a ship anchored off Hoboken—a drop of 90 feet. Each event brought Sam greater celebrity, and people began to pay to see him.

The next year, the citizens of Buffalo, New York, invited Sam to jump down Niagara Falls on October 6, 1829. Crowds gathered, but Sam failed to appear. When he showed up the next day, the crowds returned. At 4:00 P.M., Sam stood on a small platform 96 feet above the falls. He jumped, onlookers gasped . . . and then cheers went up as he was spotted swimming to safety. He repeated the feat 10 days later.

How Sam Patch Got His Muscles

When Sam was a teenager, his job at the mill required him to use his hand and knee to return, or push, the 1,568-pound carriage that held the spindles of the spinning machine. He did this four times a minute for 12 hours a day.

S AM'S NEXT challenge was the 100-foot-tall High Falls of the Genessee River in Rochester, New York. He advertised a jump on November 6, and on that day, 5,000 people gathered. Sam leaped, this time with a pet bear. But this still was not high enough. On Friday, November 13, 1829, he climbed a ladder to a platform 25 feet over the High Falls, a height of 125 feet in total.

In every previous jump, Sam had gone into the water feet first. This time, he struck the water at an angle. He never came to the surface. For weeks, rumors spread that he had not jumped but instead had dropped a dummy or that he had hid in an underwater cave and surfaced after the crowd had gone home.

But he had jumped. On March 17, 1830, his body was found down-river, where the Genesee River empties into Lake Ontario, when a farmer chopped a hole in the ice to water his horses.

DRUMMER BOYS AND GIRL SPIES

KIDS WHO FOUGHT IN THE CIVIL WAR

IN April 1865, the Civil War ended. Soldiers on both sides picked up their packs one last time and started for home. Most were men between 18 and 39 years old, but many were children.

HISTORIANS believe that as many as 100,000 Union soldiers were boys under the age of 15. (Confederate Army records are not as complete, but estimates in the South are similar.) Although the official age cutoff for enlisting was 18, recruiters looked the other way if an under-age boy signed up to serve as a drummer, bugler, messenger, or telegraph operator—all considered "noncombat" roles. However, drummers and buglers were part of every battle, their drumbeats and bugle blasts signaling soldiers to close ranks, attack, or retreat. Because many soldiers looked so youthful, girls who wanted to join the armies could successfully disguise themselves as males and sign up as soldiers. Historians have documented more than 400 cases of young girls and women who served as men.

WHO were these kids? Some were orphans, some runaways, some simply determined to follow a father or older brother to war. Because record-keeping was haphazard, no one was expected (or able) to produce a birth certificate to verify their age. And in 1861, when the war began, no one thought it would last more than a few months, so enlisting in the army may have seemed like a lark to a farm kid tired of shoveling manure or hoeing corn. Here are some of their stories:

THE YOUNGEST: Edward Black was 8 years and 10 months old when he joined the 21st Indiana Volunteers in 1861 as a drummer boy. He was captured at the Battle of Baton Rouge in August 1862 and then freed. He reenlisted in February 1863 and served until the end of the war. He was the youngest Union soldier known to have served. The youngest Confederate soldier is thought to have been Charles C. Hay, who joined an Alabama regiment when he was 11.

MEDAL OF HONOR WINNERS: Orion Howe, 14, was a drummer who volunteered to cross the battlefield at Vicksburg, Mississippi, to convey an order for some much-needed ammunition for his Union regiment. Though severely wounded, he completed his mission and earned the Medal of Honor for his bravery.

John Cook, 15, was a Union bugler who was awarded the Medal of Honor after the war for his heroism during the Battle of Antietam in September 1862, when he took the place of a dead cannoneer and helped to defend a Union position.

"DRUMMER BOY OF CHICKAMAUGA":

Johnny Clem was an under-size 11-year-old runaway from Ohio when he joined the 22nd Michigan Regiment in 1861 as a drummer and unofficial mascot. He was paid $13 a month for his services. During the Battle of Chickamauga in Georgia, Johnny reportedly picked up a gun and shot a Confederate officer, earning himself a promotion to sergeant. Johnny made the army his career, retiring as a brigadier general, and was the last Civil War veteran to serve in the army. He died in San Antonio, Texas, in 1937, and is buried in Arlington National Cemetery.

KILLED IN BATTLE:

Edwin Francis Jemison, born in Milledgeville, Georgia, enlisted at age 16 in the 2nd Louisiana Volunteer Infantry as an aide to Confederate general John Magruder. He served for 14 months before he was killed by a cannonball during the Battle of Malvern Hill in Virginia in 1862. His photograph, probably taken late in 1861, is one of the most famous portraits of the war.

"I THOUGHT OF HOME FAR AWAY. . . . I WONDERED IF MY FATE WOULD EVER BE KNOWN TO THEM."

–*Confederate soldier E. D. Patterson, age unknown*

★ ★

MASTER OF DISGUISE: Sarah Emma Edmonds of New Brunswick, Canada, ran away from an arranged marriage at age 16, dressed and spoke as a man as she made her way to the United States, and enlisted as Private Frank Thompson in the 2nd Michigan Infantry in May 1861, part of the first wave of enlistments. She spied for the Union while disguised as an Irish peddler, a young male slave, and a Confederate cavalryman. When Sarah contracted malaria in 1863, she deserted rather than submit to a medical examination and resumed life as a woman. She published her memoirs in 1864.

"DAY AFTER DAY AND NIGHT AFTER NIGHT DID WE TRAMP ALONG THE ROUGH AND DUSTY ROADS 'NEATH THE MOST BROILING SUN . . . SCARCELY STOPPING TO GATHER THE GREEN CORN FROM THE FIELDS TO SERVE US FOR RATIONS."

—Confederate soldier John Delhaney, age 16

★ ★

"SMALLEST MAN IN THE COMPANY": Jennie Hodgers, a native of County Louth, Ireland, enlisted in the 95th Illinois Infantry as Albert Cashier in 1862, when she was 19 years old. Although a fellow Union soldier remarked that Albert was the "smallest man in the company," no one questioned "his" courage during more than 40 battles. Jennie continued to live as a man after the war, and her gender was not discovered until she was hospitalized after an automobile accident in 1910 and later forced to wear a dress. When she died in 1915, her wartime comrades testified on her behalf, and she was buried in her full uniform with military honors.

LATE FOR DINNER: Elisha Stockwell was a 15-year-old farm boy from Alma, Wisconsin, whose father pulled him out of the Union Army enlistment line to tell him that he needed him to help burn charcoal (an arduous job, to be sure). Elisha went home, gathered up some clothes, and headed out for a different enlistment center. He wrote later that his sister was making dinner when he left. He recalled: "I told her I had to go downtown. She said, 'Hurry back, for dinner will soon be ready.' But I didn't get back for 2 years." Elisha marched off with 32 men from his town. In a letter posted soon after the Battle of Shiloh in 1862, he wrote, "I want to say, as we lay there and the shells were flying over us, my thoughts went back to my home, and I thought what a foolish boy I was to run away and get into such a mess as I was in. I would have been glad to have seen my father coming after me." Two years later, only three of the original 33 were still alive. Elisha and his company were marching toward Montgomery, Alabama, in 1865, when they got the news that the war had ended. The next day, he began walking back home to Wisconsin.

"THE HORRORS OF THE BATTLEFIELD WERE BROUGHT VIVIDLY BEFORE ME. I JOINED A DETACHMENT WHICH WAS COLLECTING THE DEAD FOR BURIAL. . . . THE SCENES WERE SO TERRIBLE THAT I BECAME FAINT, AND MAKING MY WAY TO A TREE, SAT DOWN, THE MOST WOEBEGONE 12-YEAR-OLD IN AMERICA."

–Fred Grant, describing the scene at Vicksburg, Mississippi, viewed while accompanying his father, then Lieutenant General and future President Ulysses S. Grant

SPIN YOUR

WOOD-BLOCK CAR RACING IS FUN!

Every year, kids from all around the country make small, gravity-powered cars from soft wood and race them on prepared tracks. Some events are organized by groups or clubs; Pinewood Derbies are held by Cub Scouts. Kids of all ages participate. With a little work (and help from an adult), you and your friends can make your own cars and compete for originality as well as speed.

WHEELS

TO MAKE YOUR OWN CAR,
you will need these supplies and tools. (Kits for making wooden cars are available online or at hobby shops and include one soft pine block, four axles, four wheels, and instructions.)

- block of soft pine or balsa wood
- saw
- sandpaper
- weights (coins, stones, fishing weights)
- paint and/or stickers
- 4 finishing nails
- dry powdered graphite, or 1 teaspoon of "pencil lead" shavings
- 4 wheels
- hammer

● Before you cut the block that will form your car, decide on its shape and design. It can be anything! Some examples are a hot dog car, a vegetable car, a cartoon character car—even a real-looking car!

● Trace the outline on the wood block. Ask an adult to cut it for you or help you do it. Sand your car until it has no rough edges.

● Weights will help your car to reach its maximum speed. Attach weights near the rear—but not on the bumper or at the end of the car. Putting weights there can cause the front of the car to lift up, sending it off course. Use glue to attach the weights under or near the rear of the car or drill holes for the weights and fit them into the holes before gluing.

● For races between you and your friends, you might want the cars to be the same weight when finished. If so, use a kitchen scale to determine the weight of each car as you make it.

● Decorate any part of your car except the wheel wells (if you have them) with paint, stickers, or other items. Paint in the wheel wells could cause friction and slow the car.

● Use a finishing nail as the axle for each wheel. To increase speed, lubricate the axles with dry powdered graphite (it comes in a small tube) or sharpen a lead pencil and then use its eraser to pick up graphite shavings and rub them onto each axle. Reapply as needed.

● Put the wheels on the axles, then tap each axle lightly with a hammer to secure it in the wood. Now you're ready to roll!

READY, SET, RACE!

The cars will roll on just about any smooth surface that provides a slope; you will also need a safe area for stopping. Your track could be a driveway, a ramp, or another homemade course. Race your cars side by side or individually, timing each one with a stopwatch.

Also give awards for car design and decoration—for example, Most Original, Most Colorful, Funniest, and Most Realistic.

WOODEN CAR WONDERS

Official wood-block car racing began in 1953. Ten-year-old Donn Murphy of Manhattan Beach, California, wanted to race in the Soapbox Derby, but he was too young. His dad, Donald Murphy, a model maker, had the idea of a race for small cars hand-built by kids. This became the Pinewood Derby. One year after the first race, the Pinewood Derby was adopted by the Boy Scouts of America, and races were held nationwide. A bronze plaque on the Scout House in Manhattan Beach commemorates the first Pinewood Derby, held on May 15, 1953.

The longest Pinewood Derby racecourse was a 12-lane, 320-foot track built by the Boston Minuteman Council and Boy Scouts of America in Boston, Massachusetts, on October 7, 2012.

GOT GAME?

Try these easy and fun contests using objects found around the house. Play against your family or friends or, where speed is a factor, by yourself against the clock anytime you have a few minutes and nothing to do.

LOONY SPOONY

Grasp a spoon by the handle and hold your arm out straight. Using your other hand, place other spoons on top, one at a time, and see how many you can hold.

EASY AS 1-2-3- . . . 4

See who's the first to find the numbers 1-2-3-4 (in that order) in a phone book.

SPIN THE MAGAZINE

Toss a magazine on the floor at least 3 feet away while spinning it sideways so that it remains flat. See who can have it spin at least once and come closest to landing "right-reading"—that is, so that the title is at the top the way it would normally be. Try spinning more than one rotation. (Get your parents' permission before tossing the magazine.)

CAN OR BOTTLE BOWLING

Use empty cans or water bottles as bowling pins with any small ball. Don't attempt to keep score or put the "pins" in a triangle. Gather as many as you can, like 20 to 30. See who can knock down the most with one roll.

SOCK SORTING

Make a pile of clean socks or two piles of equal number. See who is fastest at sorting them into matching pairs.

BASKET BALLS

Toss crumpled newspaper balls into wastebaskets. See who can get the most inside in a given amount of time.

PAGING ALL KIDS

Pick a number. See who—with eyes closed—can open a magazine or book to the page closest to the number.

THAT'S HATS

Place a canned good from the kitchen on the floor 10 feet away. Toss hats to land on top. One point for the first hat; two points if you can land a hat on top of the first; three points for three hats; etc.

AIR DROP

Place a clean empty gallon milk jug on the floor. With arm extended above, see who can drop the most pencils, dried beans, or other small objects into the jug in a given amount of time.

MEMORY MATCH

You need one set of the same 10 small objects for each contestant, plus one more for a master set. Objects can be different pieces of pasta, bottle caps, twist ties of different colors, cookies, or crackers. (For example, for three players, you would need four sets of the same 10 different things.) With contestants not looking, have someone arrange the master set of objects in a line and cover them with a dishtowel or napkin. Reveal the objects to the contestants for 10 seconds, then see which contestant can come closest to replicating the original order of the master set in a given amount of time.

LACE RACE

Untie a shoe. Remove the lace and put it on the floor. Pick it up and then re-lace and re-tie the shoe. Who can do it fastest?

ALPHABET SNOOP

See who can circle the most letters of the alphabet (one time each) in a magazine or newspaper in 10 minutes.

BEST IDEA

Make up your own game and tell everyone about it at Almanac4kids.com/TellUs/GotGames.

The Game Game

Match each term with its sport or activity.

___ **1.** Neck shot	**A.** Ski jumping
___ **2.** Hip toss	**B.** Basketball
___ **3.** Flick	**C.** Field hockey
___ **4.** Brakeman	**D.** Football
___ **5.** Lip	**E.** Horse racing
___ **6.** Nutmeg	**F.** Figure skating
___ **7.** Butterfly	**G.** Cheerleading
___ **8.** Palming	**H.** Soccer
___ **9.** Sack	**I.** Polo
___ **10.** Rail runner	**J.** Wrestling
___ **11.** Candlesticks	**K.** Bobsledding
___ **12.** Swizzle	**L.** Swimming

ANSWERS: 1. I (hitting the ball under the horse's neck); **2.** J (a throw employing a low center of gravity to roll the opponent over your body onto his back); **3.** C (a pass using enough force to make the ball rise off the ground); **4.** K (the person who sits at the back of the sled, whose role is to apply the brakes at certain parts of the course); **5.** A (the edge of the slope where the ski jumper takes off); **6.** H (to pass the ball between a player's legs); **7.** L (a symmetrical stroke with both arms carried over the water while kicking both legs as one); **8.** B (a violation in which a player moves his hand under the ball and scoops it while dribbling); **9.** D (when the quarterback is tackled behind the line of scrimmage); **10.** E (a horse that prefers to run next to the inside rail); **11.** G (a basic motion in which the cheerleader holds the arms out straight in front, with the fists facing each other, as if each were holding a candlestick); **12.** F (a technique to move forward or backward by simultaneously using the inside edges of both skates in an in-and-out fashion).

BOARD TALK

GRIND: to slide the axles along the edge or the top of an object

FAKIE: skating backward

GET ON

SLAM: to fall off your board and hurt yourself

GOOFIE: skating with your right foot forward; the opposite of "regular foot"

SHOVE-IT:

to turn the board without turning your body, so that the board spins around under your feet

BOARD!

Skateboarders have their own history, their own language—their own world.

AIR: when skateboard and skater leave the ground or ramp; short for "aerial"

OLLIE: a jump started by tapping the tail of the board with your back foot (the basis for most skateboarding tricks)

RECORD RIDES

SPEED

■ Wearing an aerodynamic suit and helmet, **Gary Hardwick** reached a record speed of nearly 63 miles per hour during a race at Fountain Hills, Arizona, on September 26, 1998.

ROTATIONS

■ **Tony Hawk** holds one of the most amazing world records. At the 1999 X Games, Tony became the first skater to land a 900—two-and-a-half rotations in midair!

SKATEBOARD FIRSTS

■ Bill Richards, owner of a surf shop in North Hollywood, California, sees some boys riding surfboards with wheels on them. He buys some wheels from a roller skate company, puts them on his surfboards, and begins selling "sidewalk surfboards."

1958

■ The Roller Derby Skateboard is introduced.

1959

JUMPS

■ **Danny Way** made skateboarding history on July 9, 2005, when he jumped over the Great Wall of China on his skateboard. He became the first person to clear the massive structure without motorized aid.

■ Danny holds the world record for longest distance jumped on a skateboard at 79 feet, which he set at the Big Air event at the 2004 X Games.

■ He also holds the record for height out of a ramp on a skateboard at 23.5 feet, which he set in 2003.

■ The first national skateboard championship is held. By now, more than 50 million skateboards have been manufactured.

■ Richard "Larry" Stevenson patents a skateboard with a kicktail—an upward curve at the back—that makes it easier to control.

■ Frank Nasworthy creates the polyurethane wheel, which provides much better traction than the old baked clay wheels.

1965

1971

1972

PET
Curiosities

What Do You Know About Dogs?

An adult dog has 42 teeth.

Dogs do see in color but not as well as humans.

About one-third to one-half of homes in America have a dog. Homes with dogs number about 43 million.

The most popular names for dogs are Bella, Max, Buddy, Lucy, and Daisy.

The only dog that does not bark is the basenji.

Most domestic dogs can run up to 19 miles per hour.

Two breeds of dog have black tongues, the chow chow and the shar-pei. All other dogs have pink tongues.

Newborn puppies can not see or hear and have no teeth.

The poodle is an accomplished swimmer; its distinctive haircut was originally meant to cover its joints and keep them warm.

The fastest dog is the greyhound, which can run up to 45 miles per hour.

Puppies should be fed three or four times per day; food should be left out for 5 to 10 minutes at a time. Older dogs can be fed twice a day.

USEFUL & AMUSING

By twitching its ears, a dog can detect the origin of sound in 6/100 of a second.

The top five favorite dog breeds are Labrador retriever, German shepherd, golden retriever, beagle, and bulldog.

A group of puppies is a litter; a group of dogs is a kennel or pack.

The oldest known dog was Bluey, an Australian cattle dog from Victoria, who lived to be 29 years, 5 months old. Most dogs live for 8 to 15 years.

Dogs sweat through the pads of their feet, not by salivating.

All About Cats

About one-third of homes in America have a cat. Homes with cats number about 36 million.

Cats are either right-pawed or left-pawed. They have five toes on each front paw but only four toes on each back paw.

All cats are born with blue eyes.

At night, cats see about six times better than humans.

A group of kittens is a kindle; a group of cats is a clowder.

Kittens up to 4 months old may need to be fed three times per day; older cats, twice a day. Some cat owners leave food out continuously, but if the food is wet and spoils, the cat will not eat it.

Cats seldom "meow" at each other; they make that sound for humans.

Cats can see color.

To help them hold prey in their mouth, cats have tiny backward hooks called papillae on their tongue.

The oldest known cat was Creme Puff of Austin, Texas, who lived to be 38 years, 3 days old.

There are about 40 different breeds of domestic cats. The most popular breed of pedigreed cat is the Persian.

Dogs and Cats Have These Things in Common

Both dogs and cats usually have four to six babies (puppies or kittens) in a litter.

Dogs can donate their blood to other dogs, and cats can donate to other cats.

Chocolate is poisonous to both dogs and cats.

Know Your Knots

- The **bight** is any part of a rope between the ends or the curved section of a rope in a knot.
- A bight becomes a **loop** when two parts of a rope cross.
- The place at which two parts of a rope meet in a loop is the **crossing point**.
- The place at which two or more loops bend is the **elbow**.
- The **working end** of a rope is the end being used to make a knot.
- The **standing end** (or standing part) of a rope is the end not involved in making a knot.

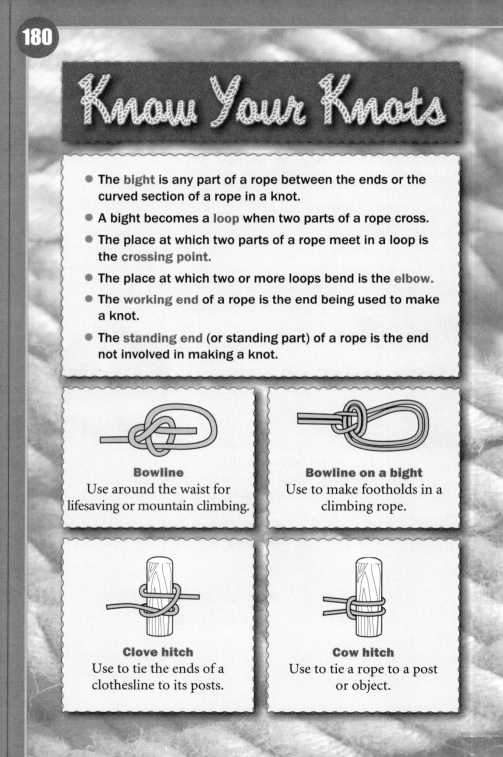

Bowline
Use around the waist for lifesaving or mountain climbing.

Bowline on a bight
Use to make footholds in a climbing rope.

Clove hitch
Use to tie the ends of a clothesline to its posts.

Cow hitch
Use to tie a rope to a post or object.

**Double sheet bend
(weaver's knot)**
Use to tie together two
ropes of different sizes
and/or materials.

Running bowline
Use to form a sliding loop.

Fisherman's knot
Use to tie two ropes together.

Sheepshank
Use to shorten a rope
without cutting it;
best on coarse,
nonsynthetic rope.

Heaving line knot
Use to add weight to the end
of a rope, making it easier
to throw ("heave").

Sheet bend
Use to join two
different-size ropes.

Overhand knot
Use to prevent a rope from
unraveling or slipping
through a ring.

Square (reef) knot
Use to bundle objects—
not ropes—together
(not always securely);
used by sailors to reduce
the area of ("reef") sails.

BIRD GROUPS

BITTERNS
sedge, siege

EAGLES
congregation, convocation

HUMMINGBIRDS
bouquet, charm, glittering, shimmer, tune

BUZZARDS
wake

FINCHES
charm

JAYS
band, party, scold

CHICKS
chattering, peep

FLAMINGOS
flamboyance, stand

LARKS
ascension, bevy, exaltation

CRANES
sedge, siege

GEESE
flock, gaggle (on ground), plump, skein (in flight), wedge (in flight)

MAGPIES
charm, gulp, murder, tiding

CROWS
congress, horde, murder

HAWKS
boil (two or more spiraling in air), cast, cauldron, kettle (in flight)

MALLARDS
brace (in flight), suit, sword

DUCKS
brace, flock (in flight), paddling, raft (on water)

HERONS
scattering, sedge, siege

NIGHTINGALES
watch

When you see two or more of these birds together, this is what they are called . . .

OWLS
parliament, study, wisdom

PLOVERS
congregation, stand,
wing (in flight)

STARLINGS
affliction, chattering,
murmuration

PARROTS
company, pandemonium

PTARMIGANS
covey

STORKS
mustering

PARTRIDGES
covey

QUAIL
bevy, covey, drift

SWANS
ballet, bevy, game,
lamentation, wedge (in flight)

PEACOCKS
muster, ostentation

RAVENS
congress, horde, murder,
unkindness

TURKEYS
flock, gang, rafter

PENGUINS
colony, crèche, huddle,
muster, parcel, rookery

ROOKS
building, clamor, parliament

WOODCOCKS
fall

PHEASANTS
nest, nide (a brood), nye

SPARROWS
host, knot, quarrel

WOODPECKERS
descent

A Happy

CAN YOU WHISTLE? People have been doing it—making music with their mouths—for thousands of years. Many people find whistling to be delightful and some people think that it's impolite, but "Big Band" members of the 1920s and '30s often included whistlers as well as musicians. Among the best-known and most popular more recent performances have been that by the dwarfs in Walt Disney's animated film *Snow White and the Seven Dwarfs,* who whistled while they worked, and the whistled theme song on television's *Andy Griffith Show.*

Today, whistling is an art, performed in international competitions as well as on the street by happy people.

Ways to Whistle

PUCKER WHISTLING

Most amateur and professional whistlers are pucker whistlers.

- Place one clean pinky finger in your mouth and use it as a guide to form the letter "O" with your lips. Remove your finger from your mouth.
- Blow, moving your tongue, teeth, and lips slightly until sound comes out of your mouth.

TOOTH WHISTLING

This involves the tongue, the roof of the mouth, and the teeth, but not the lips.

June

HAND WHISTLING

Hand whistles produce a more "hollow" sound than either the pucker or finger whistle.

■ Cup your hands snugly, fingers overlapped, and push thumb knuckles together to form a tiny hole.

■ Pucker your lips and blow into the upper half of the opening, over the knuckles.

FINGER WHISTLING

Finger whistles produce a more piercing sound than most pucker whistles. This is often the whistle for hailing a taxi.

■ Insert your pinky fingers into your mouth to control the shape and the size of the opening and to create a more forceful stream of air.

■ Blow, moving your fingers, tongue, teeth, and lips slightly until sound comes out of your mouth.

PALATAL (ROOF) WHISTLING

This rare form involves forcing air between the tongue and the roof of the mouth, moving the lips as necessary.

Practice Exercises

To keep your lips and tongue in shape, practice these exercises:

- Open your mouth. Move the tip of your tongue back and forth, touching each corner of your mouth.
- Stick out your tongue and try to touch the tip of your nose. Relax. Try to touch your tongue to the end of your chin. Relax and repeat both.
- Put your bottom lip over your top lip. Hold it for a few seconds. Then put your top lip over your bottom lip.

DID YOU KNOW?

- Students on La Gomera, one of the Canary Islands, are learning *silbo* (from the Spanish verb "to whistle"), a nearly extinct whistling language.
- People whistle to communicate in Papua New Guinea, Mexico, Vietnam, Guyana, China, Nepal, Senegal, and a few mountainous pockets in southern Europe.
- Many whistlers start by imitating birds.

Sound Advice

- Use wax-free lip balm. Wax tends to distort the sound.

- Do not eat dairy products before whistling. Milk, cheese, and yogurt can thicken the mucus in your mouth and throat.

- Avoid kissing! It can make your lips mushy.

Play Your Oven

Well, your oven rack...

An oven harp may not be a real musical instrument, but its music is so astonishing that it will amaze your family and surprise your friends (and you, too!).

1. Go to the kitchen and, with your parents' permission, remove one of the wire racks from your oven.

2. Find some string or lightweight twine, like the kind used for tying up packages. Cut off a 3-foot length of string and tie one end to a corner of the rack. Then cut and tie another length to an adjacent corner.

3. Get a volunteer to wrap the last few inches of each string around the tips of his or her little fingers, like a strand of dental floss.

4. Have your volunteer insert one string-wrapped finger into each ear (not far!) and bend forward from the waist, so that the rack hangs free of his or her body.

5. Strum lightly on the bars of the dangling oven rack with the handle of a wooden spoon.

You, the strummer, will only hear some faint plinks, but your volunteer will experience an astonishing series of echoing, bell-like tones. Don't be surprised if you both erupt into a fit of giggles. It's fun!

6. Trade places, and you'll be entertained all over again.

ACKNOWLEDGMENTS

PICTURE CREDITS

ABBREVIATIONS:
AP–Associated Press Images
FEMA–Federal Emergency
  Management Agency
GI–Getty Images
MB–Media Bakery
NASA–National Aeronautics and
  Space Administration
NOAA–National Oceanic and
  Atmospheric Administration
SS–Shutterstock
TS–Thinkstock
WM–Wikimedia

Front cover: (Nebula) NASA. (Firefighter) Bureau of Land Management/WM. (Girl, bottom) Courtesy of Jessica Carscadden. (All others) TS.

Calendar: 8–10: TS. 12: TS. 13: Becky Luigart-Stayner. 14–15: (Top) Maria Isaeva/SS. 14–15: (January) Didier Descouens/WM. (February) TS. (March) Mauro Cateb/WM. (April) TS. (May) TS. (June) TS. (July) Honored Member/SS. (August) Boykung/SS. (September) Sapphiredge/WM. (October) Dpulitzer/WM. (November) TS. (December) WM. 16: TS. 17: (Center left) Fritz Geller-Grimm/WM. (All others) TS. 18: TS. 19: (Top left) Gmoose1/WM. (Center right) DB King/WM. (Center left) TS. 20–21: TS. 22–23: TS. 24–27: TS. 28: (Top right) MB/MarketPlace. (Center right) TS. (Bottom left) TS. 29: TS.

Astronomy: 32–33: NASA. 34: (Middle) Huntington Library/SuperStock. (All others) NASA. 35: NASA. 37: (#5) New Forest Observatory. (#10) University of Arizona Mt. Lemmon Sky Center. (All others) NASA.

Weather: 38–39: TS. 40: (Top right) TS. (Center right) TS. (Bottom left) NOAA Photo Library. (Bottom center and right) WM. 41: (Top left and center left) WM. (Center right) Ian Furst/WM. (Bottom right) Böhringer Friedrich/WM. 42: (Center left) Eder Dueñas A./WM. (Top right) TS. (Bottom right) Kevin Jones/WM. 43: (Top) Drw25/WM. (Bottom) Brocken Inaglory/WM. 46–47: Bureau of Land Management/WM. 48: WM. (Bottom) WM. 49: (Left) Bureau of Land Management/WM. (Right) TS. 50: (Top left) Jeff McIntosh/AP. (Center right) WM. (Bottom right) US Fish & Wildlife Service NE Region/WM. 51: (Top left) Bidgee/WM. (Top right) David Kadlubowski/AP. (Bottom left) FEMA/WM.

In the Garden: 52: (Center right) MB. (All others) TS. 53: TS. 54: (Center left) MB. (All others) TS. 55: TS. 56–59: (Illustrations) Kim Kurki. 60–61: (Background) TS. 60: MB. 61: TS. 62–65: (Illustrations) Tim Robinson.

On the Farm: 66–69: TS. 72–73: (Illustrations) Kristin Kest.

Accomplished Kids: 74: TS. 75: (Top) Dwight Henrickson. (Bottom) Man-Cans.com. 76: TS. 77: (Top left) TS. (Center right) Mac Innes Photography/Dept. of the Taoiseach/GI. 78: (Top and center) TS. (Bottom) wristies.com. 79: (Top) Bruce Kluckhohn/GI. (Bottom) TS. 81: (Top) David Smith/The Canadian Press/AP. (Bottom) TS. 82: National Park Service. 83: Daily Echo. 84: (Top) Adolphe Pierre-Louis/The Albuquerque Journal/AP. (Bottom) TS. 85: WM. 89: Michael Nemeth.

Nature: 92: TS. 93: (Top right) Kevin Collins/WM. (Bottom left) TS. (Bottom right) Janine Forbes/WM. 94: (Top left) Lairich Rig/WM. (Bottom right) TS. 95: TS. 96–98: TS. 100: TS. 101: (Center) Mark A. Wilson/WM. (Bottom right) Hugo A. Quintero/WM. (All others) TS. 102–103: TS. 104–109: TS. 110–111: (Illustrations) Eric Ingraham. 112: TS. 113: (Top) WM. (Bottom) TS. 114: Kelvin Song/WM. 115: WM. 116: TS. 117: (Top) WM. (Bottom) TS. 118: TS. 119: Steve Goodwin/GI.

Food: 120–121: TS. 120: (Left) Maple Lodge Farms. 121: (Center) TS. 122: (Top) TS. (Bottom) Aimee Seavey. 123: (Top left and bottom left) Aimee Seavey. (Top right) ESPN Images. 124: (Center) MB. (Bottom left) TS. 125: TS. 126: (Top left) WM. (Bottom) TS. 127: (Top) Africa Studio/SS. (Center) zkruger/SS. (Bottom) Marysckin/SS. 128–133: TS. 134–137: Aimee Seavey.

Health: 138: TS. 139: (Top left and right) TS. (Bottom right) MB. 140: (Bottom left) MB/MarketPlace. (Top right and bottom right) TS. 141: TS. 142–143: TS. 144–145: TS. 146–149: (Illustrations) Tim Robinson.

Wild Adventurers: 150–157: (Illustrations) Tim Robinson.

History: 158–159: (Background) TS. 158: (Bottom) Minnesota Historical Society/WM. 159: (Top right) WM. 160–163: WM.

Sports: 164–167: (Background) TS. 164: TS. 165: (Bottom) MB. 166: TS. 167: (Top) Joe Mabel/WM. (Bottom) WM. 168–171: TS. 172–175: (Background) TS. 172–173: TS. 174: (Top left) Suzanne Cordeiro/Corbis/AP. (Bottom left and right) WM. 175: (Top left) PredatorSkates.com. (Top right) Greg Baker/AP. 175: (Bottom left) Starrfilms.com/YouTube. 175: (Bottom center and right) WM.

Useful & Amusing: 176: TS. 177: (Top right) Fugzu/WM. (All others) TS. 178–179: TS. 182: (Crow) Dick Daniels/WM. (Jay) Rob Hanson/WM. (Nightingale) Jerry Oldenettel/WM. (All others) TS. 183: (Peacock) Kabir Bakie/WM. (Plover) Mike Morel/WM. (Rook) H. Zell/WM. (Starling) Ingrid Taylar/WM. (Woodcock) Ronald Slabke/WM. (Woodpecker) Tatooeddreamer/WM. (All others) TS. 184–185: MB. 186: (Top left) MB. (Center right and bottom left) TS. 187: (Illustration) Tim Robinson.

CONTRIBUTORS

Edward Brotak: When Nature Flames Up, 46. **Jack Burnett:** Got Game?, 168. **Alice Cary:** What Happens When a Cloud Touches the Ground? Fog!, 38; Kids' Great Finds, 80; Go Buggy!, 92. **Sharon Chriscoe:** Spin Your Wheels, 164. **Mare-Anne Jarvela:** Amazing Inventions, 74; Nuts to You!, 128; The Game Game, 171; Get on Board!, 172. **Barbara Mills Lassonde:** Beware of the Bear!, 104; A Sweet Discovery, 124. **Margo Letourneau:** Grow a Hideaway, 56. **Martie Majoros:** You're a Gem!, 14; Dried Flower Delights, 60; Giving Kids, 86; The Brain: Your Own Personal Supercomputer, 138. **Susan Peery:** Drummer Boys and Girl Spies, 158. **Sarah Perreault:** Why Do We Leap Years?, 22; How Animals Catch Their Zzzzzzzzs, 100; Let's Do Lunch, 134; That's Gross! No, It's Snot, 146. **Stephanie Shaw:** The Farmer and the Rat, 72. **Janice Stillman:** The Newest Eye in the Sky, 32; Oh, My Stars!, 36; Farmers' Market Fun Facts, 66; He Walked on Air, 154; Pet Curiosities, 176. **Heidi Stonehill:** It's a Blast!, 112.

Content not cited here is adapted from *The Old Farmer's Almanac* archives or appears in the public domain. Every effort has been made to attribute all material correctly. If any errors have been unwittingly committed, they will be corrected in a future edition.

INDEX

ACTIVITIES

Look for our next edition of _The Old Farmer's Almanac for Kids_ coming your way in September 2017!